LOVE IN THE RUINS

MODERN CATHOLICS IN SEARCH OF THE ANCIENT FAITH

LOVE IN THE RUINS

MODERN CATHOLICS IN SEARCH OF THE ANCIENT FAITH

Edited by Anne M. Larson

ANGELUS PRESS
2915 FOREST AVENUE
KANSAS CITY, MISSOURI 64109

"Front Row Seat to the Revolution" by John Vennari, "Shadow Sacraments" by Dr. David Allen White, "The Gate Called the Beautiful" and "From Hoboken to Eternity" by John Rao edited by Angelus Press. Angelus Press does not necessarily endorse all the views of the authors.

Library of Congress Cataloging-in-Publication Data

Love in the ruins : modern Catholics in search of the ancient faith / edited by Anne M. Larson.
   p. cm.
ISBN 978-1-892331-66-3
1. Mass. 2. Catholic traditionalist movement. I. Larson, Anne M., 1962-

BX2230.3.L68 2009
264'.02036--dc22

2009000414

©2009 by Angelus Press
All rights reserved. No part of this book may be reproduced or transmitted in any form or by any means, electronic or mechanical, including photocopying, recording, or by any information storage and retrieval systems without permission in writing from the publisher, except by a reviewer, who may quote brief passages in a review.

ANGELUS PRESS
2915 FOREST AVENUE
KANSAS CITY, MISSOURI 64109
PHONE (816) 753-3150
FAX (816) 753-3557
ORDER LINE 1-800-966-7337
WWW.ANGELUSPRESS.ORG

ISBN 978-1-892331-66-3
FIRST PRINTING—March 2009

Printed in the United States of America

Contents

Preface 1

Joseph O'Brien 3
A First Reckoning with the Latin Mass

Michael Larson 11
Waking Up Catholic

Mary Ann Kreitzer 27
Weathering the Storm:
A Catholic's Journey from Chaos to Hope

John Vennari 39
A Front-Row Seat to the Revolution

Dr. Andrew Childs 53
Breaking the Silence: A Conversion to Truth through Music

Dr. David Allen White 71
"Shadow" Sacraments

Richard Cowden Guido 83
Day of the Locust

Dr. John C. Rao 97
From Hoboken to Eternity: The Value of Catholic
Traditionalism in the Life of One Traditionalist

Edwin Faust 113
Lost and Found

T. Renee Kozinski 129
Veronica

Michael J. Matt 141
It's the Mass that Matters!

Brian Douglass 153
Views Along the Road to Tradition

Anonymous 161
The Gate Called the Beautiful

Kenton Craven 169
In the Sacred Cave

Preface

Nearly five years ago I attended the Tridentine Latin Mass for the first time. In an incense-filled moment, I found the Faith that shaped Western Civilization and changed the course of human history. It seemed like an altogether different religion from much of mainstream Catholicism, which had been ravaged by sex scandals, declining vocations, liturgical abuse, heretical catechesis, cafeteria Catholicism, loss of faith, and more; a disturbing but undeniable reality for a Protestant who had converted to the One, Holy, Catholic, and Apostolic Church; a Church that had been radically altered in the brief span of my own lifetime. The Latin Mass and the teaching and practices emanating from it (sometimes called "traditional Catholicism") were the means by which I discovered the fullness of my Catholic Faith, which had until then been obscured from my view.

Every Catholic who has found refuge in the traditions of the Church has a story. One doesn't end up at the Latin Mass by accident. When I was making the transition to traditional Catholicism, stories of how other people had found their way to the Latin Mass fascinated me—and still do. Their stories helped me to articulate my own experience and make sense of the confusing ecclesiastical landscape. Thus the idea for this book was born.

The narratives that follow are written by Roman Catholics who have discovered or rediscovered the riches of the ancient liturgy and traditions of Holy Mother Church, powerful anecdotes to the ecclesiastic and liturgical crises of our day. They are accounts of conversion, "reversion," and simple fidelity to the Faith throughout the religious and cultural upheaval that followed in the wake of Vatican II. Many of the contributors to this book suffered for years from theological dissent and liturgical abuse in their parishes, parochial schools, and Catholic universities; some

Love in the Ruins

grew up in tradition but refused to participate in the post-conciliar revolution; some, like me, were converts to the Faith; and all were inexplicably drawn to the beauty and mystery, the truth and holiness of the centuries-old sacrifice of the Mass. Perhaps most importantly, these are stories of what Evelyn Waugh has called the "operation of Grace…the unmerited and unilateral act of love by which God continually calls souls to Himself."

Many thanks to my daughter, Kate, for her invaluable editorial assistance, to my family for their encouragement and support, and to the contributors for sharing their stories.

Anne M. Larson

Joseph O'Brien

A First Reckoning with the Latin Mass

> Now in the morning Mass you do all that the race needs to do and has done for all these ages where religion was concerned; there you have the sacred and separate Enclosure, the Altar, the Priest in his Vestments, the set ritual, the ancient and hierarchic tongue, and all that your nature cries out for in the matter of worship.
> –Hilaire Belloc, *The Path to Rome*

It is not often that one has a chance in life to experience a moment that brings into focus all the dimensions of one's Catholic faith–its height, depth, width and breadth. For me, that moment came when I assisted at my first Latin Mass–otherwise known as the Mass According to the Rite of 1962 (or more commonly as the Tridentine Mass). I grew up a typical "cradle Catholic" in the wake of the Second Vatican Council and the subsequent dismantling of Catholic culture, with only my parents' say-so that the Latin Mass ever even existed. For me, growing up Catholic involved no more and no less than the comfortable notions of the faith that accompanied me all the days of my adolescence and early adulthood. In my school-days, Catholicism was a matter of generic adherence, not of particular assent (nor the attendant suffering which Christ promised such assent would involve (cf. Mt. 10:16-23)).

This all changed, though, once I left home. Except for a brief, forgettable stint at a state university, I spent my college days steeped in Catholicism by attending Thomas Aquinas College (TAC) in Santa Paula, California. With a Great Books curriculum, TAC sought to nourish its students on the substance of real intellectual formation–theology, philosophy, literature, science, and mathematics—as taught by the literary architects of Western Civilization, that is, Aquinas, Augustine, Aristotle, Euclid, Homer, Plato, and so on. The school also places a rigorous emphasis on learning the tongue of Mother Church: Latin. This particular fact becomes important to one's spiritual life at TAC because the Mass—whether *Novus Ordo* or 1962—is celebrated exclusively in Latin. Unless you know your Latin (two years of it, starting Freshman year), your participation in the Mass is reduced to scurrying through the bilingual missal which the college provided to keep up with priest and faithful.

When I was there, Mass was celebrated in the tiny little chapel tucked away in the corner of the college commons hall. (The school is now building a downright majestic place of worship—a full-fledged chapel of traditional design—much more suitable for God and man.) The Latin Mass was celebrated the last Sunday of the month by permission of the ordinary under whose jurisdiction the college operates. Before ever having attended the Latin Mass, I had heard good things and bad things about it. But as I beheld the humble nobility of the actual thing for the first time, polemics on either side seemed to fall away like scales.

"I tell you a mystery," said Christ. So, for me, did the Latin Mass. It was steeped in mystery—the way that a Mozart composition is steeped in music or a Shakespeare play steeped in poetry. The two could not be separated without doing damage to both. But that was not all: its beauty was enticing and its intrigue was irresistible. It almost instantly garnered my respect and it certainly commanded my attention. But I suppose it was the strange mixture of fear and joy which kept my soul and senses rapt—sort of a cross between Moses' trembling awestruck before the burning bush and St. Peter eager to set up camp on Mt. Tabor after Christ's transfiguration. Truly it was "good to be here," as St. Peter said to Christ among the heavenly booths. It was sometime later, in fact, that I found words to describe my growing devotion to the Latin Mass.

In his book *The Path to Rome*, Hilaire Belloc speaks of the joys of attending daily morning Mass on his walking pilgrimage from his native France to Rome. His account shows what itch the Latin Mass was scratching for this cradle Catholic. "Of course there is a grace and influence belonging to [attending daily Mass]," Belloc states, "but it is not of that I am speaking but of the pleasing sensation of order and accomplishment which attaches to a day one has opened by Mass; a purely temporal and, for all I know, what the monks back at the ironworks would have called a carnal feeling, but a source of continual comfort to me." The Latin Mass is a nearly total immersion in mystery, a nearly beatific encounter with the heart of faith, love, and hope, and an intricate recognition of my own subordination as simple creature before simple Creator.

But Belloc makes clear that a desire for this same encounter has been hankering in the human soul since Adam and Eve first fled east of Eden. He points out that "for half an hour just at the opening of the day you are silent and recollected, and have to put off cares, interests, and passions in the repetition of a familiar action. This must certainly be a great benefit to the body and give it tone." Full participation in the Mass does not exclude the possibility of silent prayer—even long stretches of silent prayer—as part of the soul's daily spiritual diet and exercise. This, in fact, was one of the first things about the Mass that became apparent to me. The hush is not forced nor sterile nor awkward. The swish of vestments, the whispered prayers, even the breathing of those attending and participating seem to increase the mystery and give it a gravity found nowhere else on earth. Indeed when else is there so much of life packed with so much quiet? It is always so when one spends time with a loved one. So too with Christ.

Along with the quiet is the familiar routine of Mass itself—always the same, no surprises. But the sameness of the Mass no more suggests stagnation than the quietness does. After all, men of good will wish each other a good day in the same way, day after day, never doubting for a minute the importance of such a gesture, nor the benefit of such a routine. Thus, the opening salvo of prayers at Mass reminds the faithful that our God is a personal God—that He can be spoken of personally and spoken to personally: *Suscipe, sancte Pater, omnipotens aeterne Deus, hanc immaculatam hostiam, quam ego indignus famulus tuus offero tibi Deo meo vivo et vero.... Deus, qui humanae substantiae dignitatem mirabiliter condidisti et mirabilius reformasti: da nobis... Veni, sanctificator, omnipotens aeterne Deus...* ("Receive, O holy Father, almighty and eternal God, this spotless host, which I, Your unworthy servant, offer to You, my living and true God... O God, who in a wonderful manner created and ennobled human nature and still more wonderfully renewed it... Come, almighty Sanctifier and everliving God..."), and so forth. What's more, when I pray these prayers in the silence of my heart with the priest, I imagine the repetition working like drops of water constantly wearing away at the detritus that time and my sins had worked on my soul while at the same time washing over my soul and waking it to grace. As another example of effective repetition in Mass, the twice-told *Confiteor* in Mass works like a one-two punch to pride, allowing me to recollect my less-than-perfect place in the world, a little higher than the animals, a little lower than the angels, and sinful from stem to stern, helpless without the help of God. There is an equally welcomed repetition from Mass to Mass, as well. The Final Gospel–St. John's lyrical prologue–spells out the paradoxes of our faith: *In principio erat Verbum, et Verbum erat apud Deum, et Deus erat Verbum...* ("In the beginning was the Word, and the Word was with God, and the Word was God..."). Often I leave Mass thinking of T. S. Eliot's famous tag line in his deeply religious *Four Quartets*: "In my end is my beginning....In my beginning is my end." The final Gospel is a constant reminder that, as I head back to the world of men, only two terms matter in the end: Alpha and Omega.

But in this repetition of prayer and action, Belloc also sees the natural element of ritual tugging at every human heart.

> ...the Mass is a careful and rapid ritual. Now it is the function of all ritual (as we see in games, social arrangements and so forth) to relieve the mind by so much of responsibility and initiative and to catch you up (as it were) into itself, leading your life for you during the time it lasts. In this way you experience singular repose, after which fallowness I am sure one is fitter for action and judgment.

Indeed, there is an easy current along which the soul is carried when it reaches the well-practiced and familiar ritual of the Mass. The Mass is the Mass is the Mass, and the prayers themselves reflect the importance of the "careful and rapid ritual" of the Mass. *Hanc igitur oblationem servitutis nostrae, sed et cunctae familiae tuae, quaesumus, Domine, ut placatus accipias: diesque nostros in tua pace disponas, atque ab aeterna damnatione nos eripi, et in electorum tuorum jubeas grege numerari.* ("This, then, is our dutiful offering which we, Your servants and Your whole family, make to You, Lord, entreating You to accept it with favour. Order our days in Your peace, and cause us to be saved from everlasting doom and to be numbered among Your chosen ones.") Thus we pray and understand why we pray at the same time. If sin darkens the intellect even as it slowly disables the soul, then surely, as Belloc suggests, the Mass helps one sift through that darkness, to draw closer to the light, the mysteries of our faith, and the source of all mystery. The helps to this source are in the ritual—even as the river is helped along its course to the sea by the "ritual" of its banks.

But the Mass for Belloc is not just ritual—it is also a culture of sorts, a culture which demonstrates its own benefits.

> ...the surroundings [of Mass] incline you to good and reasonable thoughts, and for the moment deaden the rasp and jar of that busy wickedness which both working in one's self and received from others is the true source of all human miseries. Thus the time spent in Mass is like a short repose in a deep and well-built library, into which no sounds come and where you feel yourself secure against the outer world.

The "library" of the Mass is one that teaches even as it edifies. Prayers in the Mass can sometimes take the shape of miniature theology lessons. The Mass imparts such knowledge as has been culled by Tradition and Holy Writ—and delivers it to the faithful in digestible portions. Thus, there are angels in the architect of the Mass prayers: *Supplices te rogamus, omnipotens Deus: jube haec perferri per manus sancti Angeli tui in sublime altare tuum...* ("We humbly implore You, almighty God, bid these offering to be carried by the hands of Your holy angel to Your altar on high..."); and constant reminders that the offering made at Mass is the same as that of God's chosen bloodline of faith: *justi Abel* ("of…Abel the righteous"), *Patriarchae nostri Abrahae* ("of our father Abraham") and *summus sacerdos tuus Melchisedech* ("Melchisedech, Your high priest"). There's even a user's guide of sorts for the Eucharist: *Perceptio Corporis tui, Domine Jesu Christe, quod ego indignus sumere praesumo, non mihi proveniat in judicium et condemnationem: sed pro tua pietate prosit mihi ad tutamentum mentis et corporis, et ad medelam percipiendam…* ("Let not the partaking of Your Body, O Lord Jesus Christ, which I, though unworthy, presume to receive, turn to my judgment and condemnation; but through Your goodness may it be unto me a safeguard and a healing remedy both of soul and body…").

In Mass, the intellect is edified even as the soul is nourished. But there should be no surprise that this is so: Catholic culture has always had a broad base of appeal. William Shakespeare staged his works at the Globe Theatre to mirror the globe of human action–everyone from kings and queens to peasants and smiths those same people who were willing to pay to see the Bard's latest production. In a more profound way, the Mass provides a platform for worship with something for everyone. Far from being alien and strangely inaccessible, the Latin Mass is at bottom a thoroughly human act. Not easily obtained, for sure, anymore than Mount Tabor was easily obtained by Peter, James, and John–or Mount Calvary by their Master. But this is precisely what Belloc and the Latin Mass point to: that worship is by nature vertical, and mankind's fallen (horizontal) nature must struggle to align itself with such worship to achieve spiritual progress. The struggle does not make such worship any less human–it makes it wholly human.

In his own contemplation of the worship act, Belloc notes that by attending daily Mass

> you are doing what the human race has done for thousands upon thousands upon thousands of years. This a matter of such moment that I am astonished people hear of it so little. Whatever is buried right into our blood from immemorial habit, that we must be certain to do if we are to be fairly happy (of course no grown man or woman can really be very

happy for long, but I mean reasonably happy), and, what is more important, decent and secure of our souls.

It is not for nothing that we call the Mass a perfect sacrifice. Thus, by Belloc's reckoning, we should be perfectly happy (or at least perfectly "reasonably happy") at Mass. To attend Mass, as many a saint would vouch, is nothing short of mingling with the angels.

But curiously, the Latin Mass is not highbrow. It is a mixture of the refined and primitive. Despite the modern (and modernist) tendency to think that something in a "foreign" language (*i.e.*, Latin, the "native" language of Catholics) is somehow beyond the common scope, this product of a millennium's worth of inspired blood, sweat, and grief has endured as much for the peasant as for the king. It is a ritual with complexity of structure and sense, but it also answers a basic human need. The desire to worship, to sacrifice to that Greater Being Whom only the fool in his heart would eschew, that is something not only "built into our blood" but, since communion with Christ is the goal of the Mass, it is also built on human blood which was shed for all of mankind. Sacrifice, Belloc points out, has always been the primary mode of communicating with the mysteries of life. The holy sacrifice of the Mass, then, is the primary mode by which Catholics communicate with the Mystery Who Is Life–Jesus Christ.

Of course, it doesn't take Belloc to show us that this is the case. If I knew nothing else after attending my first Latin Mass, I knew that I was touching the heart of this mystery–and man can come no closer this side of paradise. And so, I come back to the smells and bells of that first Mass, and kneel again at the words in "The Last Gospel": *ET VERBUM CARO FACTUM EST, et habitavit in nobis...* ("AND THE WORD WAS MADE FLESH, and dwelt among us..."). Yes, Christ came to dwell among us, and dwells at the heart of our worship in the Holy Sacrifice of the Mass, an act which is every bit as human as Christ Himself.

A published poet, husband and father, Joseph O'Brien is a free-lance writer. With his wife Cecilia, he has seven children: Barbara, Seamus,

Love in the Ruins

Bernadette, Norah, Liam, Anastasia, and Mara Naomi. After transferring from TAC in his junior year, he received his bachelor's in English Literature from the University of Dallas in 1995, and a master's in English Literature in May 2003. An earlier version of this essay appeared in *Lauda, Jerusalem!* the official newsletter of the Canons Regular of the New Jerusalem, and in the October 2005 issue of the *New Oxford Review*, 1069 Kains Avenue, Berkeley CA 94706, U.S.A., and is reprinted with permission.

Michael Larson

Waking Up Catholic

A conversion story, like any story, is something of a reconstruction, limited by the clues available to one presently and by the gulf of time. Just as one cannot step into the same river twice, neither can one see with the same eyes one had at some previous point in life. What follows then is my reconstruction of the path by which I have become a traditional Roman Catholic. When I look back now, even with the illumination of hindsight, I cannot apprehend in one glance—or even in many glances—the whole of it. I see in the distance where the trail begins and bits of sunlit footpath between there and here, but much of it remains in obscurity. These are the limitations of human memory and understanding. Nevertheless I find myself here now—and for poignant reasons, which I will try to explain.

Leaving Protestantism

It seems logical that any convert might have two internal forces at work: the movement away from one thing and the movement toward something else. This was certainly the case for me in 1989 when I converted to the Catholic Church. For two years prior, I had been moving toward Catholicism, and for several years before that, I had been moving away from Protestantism. To understand more precisely the nature of this movement away, I must make clear what it was not: it was not a movement away from belief.

I was born into a Lutheran home and baptized as an infant. I was taught at a very young age by my parents to believe in the Trinity, the Incarnation, the Crucifixion, and the Resurrection. My parents also made clear to me that Christ died for my sins and that if I would accept Him as my lord and savior, He would live in my heart in this life and take me to heaven in the next. I have never stopped believing any of these things. Then again, these things cannot rightly be attributed to Protestantism, at least not in their ultimate origin. These beliefs, understood generally, are truths the Protestant reformers took with them when they broke away from the Church and started their own versions of Christianity.

Even today, most serious Catholics and Protestants would agree on these basic tenets of the faith. The disagreement would come in defining what is meant by accepting Christ as Lord and Savior, what is involved in such a proposition. What is involved for the Protestant is primarily the maintenance of belief, the perpetual mental acknowledgement, so to speak, of Christ's mastery over us and His saving love for us. In its most extreme form, this emphasis among Protestants on mental assent is essentially the principle of *sola fide* (*i.e.*, by faith alone we are saved). Here the Protestant uses the term, "faith," not as the Catholic uses it to refer to all the Articles of Faith held inviolable by the Church and to which all Catholics by definition must assent, but rather as the singular belief in Christ as Lord. The natural consequence of *sola fide* is the invisible church. To most, if not all, of the Protestants I have known, the denominations of Christianity (of which they perceive Catholicism to be merely one of many) are each a construct of man. The thinking goes like this: God alone knows which individuals from among all the denominations have belief in Jesus, the Christ. It is this group of individuals who make up the invisible church—invisible in the sense that it does not conform to any particular set of human-defined doctrines and obligations but is rather a society of like-minded believers who cross sectarian lines.

In short, these believers are one in their acceptance of Christ as Lord; the denominational disagreements about other areas of doctrine and spiritual life are considered peripheral: after all, no one denomination has all the correct answers, so one must choose a church based on one's personal preferences regarding a particular style of worship or a particular doctrinal emphasis. Many of the Protestants I know will readily acknowledge that their version of Christianity may in fact have some errors, yet they feel that there is no way to know for certain what those errors are. They reference St. Paul and say that in this life, we are left to see through the glass darkly; in the next life, God will show us where we were wrong, and only then will we all see the truths of Heaven. The implication, of course, in this kind of thinking is that the Kingdom of Heaven has not yet been revealed. Yes, we know that Christ is Lord, but universal revelation, in effect, ends there. All the rest—all other matters of doctrine, worship, and spiritual life—are up for grabs, and people, being as they are, will find endlessly different ways to adapt their religion to themselves.

In this invisible church, one's spiritual journey is, almost by necessity, a private and individualistic affair. There are many thousands of Protestant denominations, no two of them holding all matters of doctrine and religious practice in common. An individual might not even agree with certain of the doctrinal teachings or the moral obligations within his own denomination, let alone with those of another denomination. One's spiritual life, then, is one's own. Transformation, or sanctification, occurs largely in isolation. And the specific nature of what must be accomplished in this journey is rarely, if ever, articulated among Protestant thinkers. (Luther even denies the notion entirely. For him, there is no journey, no transformation. As he once put it, one remains a "dung heap" underneath, clothed with the snow-white mantle of Christ.)

This is in sharp contrast to the Catholic act of accepting Christ as Lord and Savior, which, in addition to the maintenance of one's belief, involves a public submission to the very concrete teachings and precepts of the Church, an ancient and visible society. Transformation of the individual Catholic—an absolute necessity for salvation—is the normal work of the Church, through the graces received in the seven sacraments (especially the Eucharist), through conformance to the teachings (both doctrinal and moral) of the Magisterium, through prayer (especially the Mass), and through penance. To be saved, the Catholic must, in the words of our Lord, "become perfect even as your Father in heaven is perfect." If transformation for one in a state of grace is not complete in this life, then purgatory—a final purifying fire—follows until that soul is truly made ready for heaven. But I get ahead of myself. I mention these Catholic characteristics here only in an effort to more vividly render—by way of contrast—my understanding of the Protestantism with which I had grown up.

My movement away, then, from my Protestant upbringing was not exactly a rejection of belief, at least not at the most elemental level. Rather, I was rejecting what I had come to see as a kind of impotency, an apparent powerlessness within the churches I attended, to transform practitioners—that and a general ambiguity about what such transformation might involve, how it might be accomplished. Certainly, I was powerless to change myself—this was all too clear—but even more alarming was the inability of the local church to help. In other words, I had come to perceive churchgoing as an exercise in futility: we, most of us, agreed that we needed Christ to save us, but all we could find at church was each other, men and women and children doing their best, many of them, to be kind and helpful, to say wise and sometimes meaningful things, to try together to figure out what this or that passage of Scripture might mean, to remind each other of our need for Christ, *etc.* And that was it. We shared belief (at least one main one), and we offered each other ourselves (to a limited degree), because that is all we had to offer.

Some might ask, "Well, what more do you want?" And indeed, in the realm of natural goodness, such an image of human fellowship does in fact seem touching, almost even as if it should be enough. But it is not enough. And by the age of twenty, I had figured this out: in the best of Protestant churches, there is natural goodness—sincere, well-meaning, supportive communities of those who share a belief in the need for Christ—and in the worst of them, there is chaos. But in none of them that I could see was there a supernatural reason to go to church on Sunday morning. And my exposure to various denominations had not exactly been narrow: Lutheran, as I have mentioned, but also Evangelical Free, Evangelical Covenant, Presbyterian, Baptist, Church of Christ, some independent Bible-based fundamentalist churches, and a couple varieties of Pentecostalism.

Often there were pastors with charismatic personalities or good public speaking skills; sometimes there were exceptionally nice families or a good youth group; occasionally there was what people perceived to be good biblical teaching; and in the Pentecostal churches there were signs and wonders: people speaking in tongues, people making prophecies, and people seeking (and sometimes claiming) physical healing. What I could not find in any of these churches was anything other than a lateral orientation. By that I mean a human orientation, a method of choosing and attending a church based on human issues. If the pastor was charismatic or a good speaker, we were charmed. By him! If there were nice families, we were charmed by them. If there was a good youth group, we kids were excited by the prospect of new friends. If there was what we believed to be good biblical teaching, then we were ultimately pleased with ourselves, for who else but we could determine what was good and what was errant? And if there were signs and wonders, we were either skeptical of or impressed by those claiming the sign or the wonder, and never to my recollection did such charged displays ever turn our orientation vertical. There was always too much of the individual and not enough of the individual's Maker.

During and after college (a private evangelical school), I continued to attend various churches occasionally but always with dismay. Although I could not have articulated it then, I was quite weary with myself; and the rest of humanity, I am sad to say, resides in roughly the same range as I. The Protestant churches I attended knew only how to serve me up something (or someone) slightly better or worse than myself. It became grimly clear to me that I could do as well on my own. What need had I, a blind man, to be led around by those with similar visual impairment?

So I moved away. By which I mean that I went to church less and less. I never stopped believing in those basic tenets I had learned early in life, but I had come to realize that those tenets and church attendance (at least in the churches with which I was familiar) had almost nothing in common. The tenets–Trinity, Incarnation, Crucifixion, Resurrection, Salvation, Heaven–all of them had to do with things beyond the human domain. It was the upward sweep of those realities, the vertical orientation they invited, that caused me to reject the notion of Protestant church-going long before I ever seriously considered the claims of the Catholic Church. In short, I wanted away from a lateral religion–from such inordinate preoccupation with ourselves–and a way into what is infinitely higher and grander than even the very best of what we have to offer each other.

Trying to Find Catholicism

It is beauty, I think, that lured me at last into the Catholic Church. I am artistic by nature (poet, writer, musician), so I am particularly susceptible to beauty. Often this has been to my detriment. I have sought beauty in many of its natural forms–in the drama and variety of earth's landscapes, in the human trail of art and architecture, in the drug of music, in the bond of friendship, in the love of a woman and the loveliness of her form, even (I am amused to say) in some brilliant corner of myself. In myself I could not find it; in romantic love, it is pressed; in friendship, it is by necessity limited and often ends up fading; in music, at least in popular music, it disorients; in art, it is a rabbit hole; in landscapes, it is tantalizingly inaccessible. In Catholicism, too, I would see beauty. And this was cause for both enchantment and anxiety. Would I find behind her doors the answer to all my longings, or would the Church end up merely another of beauty's tricks?

In 1987, when I was in graduate school at St. Cloud State University, I made two friends who had been raised Protestant but who were in the process of becoming Catholic. I had never heard of such a thing; my parents were not what I would call anti-Catholic, but neither was it something to take seriously in our household. My converting friends and I talked long into many nights. We argued some, but not much. My wife and I read books like *Evangelical Is Not Enough* by Thomas Howard and *Evangelicals on the Canterbury Trail* by Robert Webber, *The New Catholics*, a collection of modern conversion stories, and two books by G. K. Chesterton: *Orthodoxy* and *The Everlasting Man*. I took interest also in the fact that some of my favorite novelists were Catholic: Walker Percy, Graham Greene, and Flannery O'Connor. I would like to say that my conversion was intellectual, that pure, unadulterated reason led me to the Catholic Church. It did not. If I were to convert now, I venture to think that it would be for reasons of reason. But at that time, as a young man, I was almost entirely intuitive in my decision making.

What my intuition told me in those days, even before I had attended a single Mass, was that the Church is "lovely, dark, and deep." Frost applied these words to a patch of woods, but there was something about Catholic Christianity also that promised of regions hitherto unknown. It was the "further up and further in" described by C. S. Lewis, ironically a Protestant, in *The Chronicles of Narnia*. It was the mythopoeic rendering of purgatory, namelessly portrayed by George MacDonald, another Protestant, in a book called *Lilith*, which had affected me deeply. It was the real-world equivalent of the Middle Earth of J. R. R. Tolkein, a friend of Lewis's and the lone Catholic among my favorite fantasy authors.

From all that I had read, discussed, and intuited about Catholicism, I perceived something truly beautiful, something far beyond myself, some deep, majestic, elevated realm. There are actually many elements of the Church that fulfill these descriptors, but perhaps the easiest for new Catholics to grasp, and certainly the most important, is the Eucharist. If we are to be made perfect, even as our Father in heaven is perfect, we must be visited regularly by His Son, who is of the same essence. This happens in the Catholic Mass. The priest, standing in the stead of Christ, offers to the Father the perfect sacrifice of the Son, whereby at the consecration, the bread and wine become the Body and Blood of our Lord, who–just as He did through the Incarnation–enters our world, our very bodies, and sustains us with His supernatural life.

To my knowledge, not a single Protestant church has ever made such a claim. Instead they speak of abstractions like commemoration (popular in the free churches) or consubstantiation (the Lutheran term), whereby Christ is described as vaguely present "in and around" the bread and wine (or grape juice). I suspect these Protestant ceremonies do have value, at least for those who care to concentrate, but only in the natural realm. And they are not sacraments. They are not administered by a priest with apostolic lineage. They are not to be equated with the literal descent of Christ, who feeds His sheep with a supernatural food. Indeed, the Protestant mind is scandalized by such a notion, as were the Jews, as were His own disciples until much later, after the Ascension and the Descent of the Holy Ghost.

My apprehension of the shocking claim of the Catholic sacrament of Holy Communion was a clear and tangible pull. Again, I could not have articulated it at the time, but in this sacrament was the antithesis of all that had made me weary in the Protestant churches. Instead of a Protestant minister's private interpretation of Scripture, however astute, I was to receive Christ Himself. Instead of the well-meaning well-wishes of my fellow man, I was to receive Christ. Instead of a fine soloist, instead of the entertaining psycho-babble of a good midweek speaker, instead of a sincere Bible study, instead of a friendly potluck dinner, I was to receive Christ. "Apart from Me, you can do nothing." He truly meant these words. We are spirit and matter. In the Eucharist, we receive spiritual food but in a material form. In the Mass, in every Mass, and especially in the Eucharist, the central tenets of the Faith are elevated once again for the faithful to see: the second person of the Trinity, in His great love for the Father, is offered as a sacrifice, through which the faithful are then fed and spiritual life is perpetually resurrected. Apart from Me, you can do nothing. Church, if it is of supernatural origin, must be founded entirely, without any deviance, on these words of our Lord. I began to believe that I had found such a church.

Of course, there were other attractions: Mary and the Saints, those of my species, those who had passed through the same frailties into perfection and holiness, and were consequently far above me yet accessible through prayer; the nine choirs of Angels, those of a different species, again, far above me yet, again, accessible through prayer; the religious—priests and bishops, monks and nuns—those in this life who give up everything for the sake of Christ; the magnificent deposit of faith, the writings of the Fathers, the Popes, the Councils, *etc.*; basically, I found in Catholicism a whole hierarchical universe, most of which was well above me, and I was only too happy to take my modest place in such a grand reality. There was a kind of lifting of the Protestant ceiling, and what I beheld above me was nothing but Beauty, stretching away into eternity.

Beauty's Trick

What I have described about Catholicism is true. Every bit of it truly exists. But it is a trick of beauty to be elusive, and when I actually came to embrace the Bride of Christ, I had trouble finding her. The Church I had read about, thought about, talked about, dreamed about for two years was not the one I found when I entered the doors. Imagine my surprise. I knew, for instance, the Catholic teaching on the Eucharist—it had played a big part in my conversion—yet the liturgy I encountered seemed to downplay its significance. The priest, facing the people and speaking in the vernacular, often seemed compelled to impart his particular personality on the event—nothing blatant usually, just the nuance of facial expressions, cadence, vocal inflection, gestures. I found myself naturally focusing on the individuality of that person, the priest, rather than on Christ, who was in reality the Victim being offered to His Father. Furthermore, there was a strong feeling of informality about what was going on, perhaps best encapsulated by the inevitable trooping up of laypeople, often strangely dressed, to help the priest distribute the sacrament. This misery was topped off by the faithful, myself included, receiving our Lord in the palms of their hands, then popping Him into their mouths like fish crackers.

Love in the Ruins

I did not know, at the time, what this incomprehensible moment ought to look like, but I did know that the casual air with which we all received the Body of Christ was something of a disappointment. It took me right out of the hierarchical realm of majesty that I had long anticipated and left me once again focusing on my fellow man. Although I had become a Catholic, I found myself suffering a mysterious and demoralizing hangover from Protestant days: yes, the Catholic Church taught that the Host was truly the Body and Blood of our Lord, but even to my freshly converted eyes, nothing about the way the sacrament was handled seemed to align with that teaching.

The problem, I think, with such liturgical and rubrical informality is that doctrine is inevitably compromised as well. For priest and laity alike, the week-after-week (or day-after-day in the case of the priest) effect is to lose faith in what is actually happening. And to lose faith in the transubstantiation of the bread and wine into the Body and Blood of our Lord is to lose the entirety of the Catholic Faith. This is not an overstatement. Without a true, deep, reverent understanding of Christ's material presence in and among us, sustaining us, transforming us—without that, we as Catholics have no faith. Christ said as much:

> Amen, amen, I say to you: Unless you eat the flesh of the Son of man, and drink his blood, you shall not have life in you. He that eateth my flesh, and drinketh my blood, hath everlasting life: and I will raise him up at the last day. For my flesh, is meat indeed: and my blood, is drink indeed: He that eateth my flesh, and drinketh my blood, abideth in me, and I in him. As the living Father hath sent me, and I live by the Father: so he that eateth me, the same also shall live by me. This is the bread that came down from heaven. Not as your fathers did eat manna, and died. He that eateth this bread, shall live for ever. (John 6:54-59, Douay-Rheims)

Once this central truth is compromised in the Catholic mind, then every other article of faith is likewise undermined, because everything, every single thing that Catholics believe, is predicated on the centrality of Christ in our midst. Take that away, and all we have left is a smorgasbord of beliefs, mere mental constructs sustained by our own human powers of concentration. This is no different from what Protestants have. Without the absolute, literal centrality of Christ, the Church is neither One nor Holy nor Catholic nor even Apostolic, for it was He, Christ, who instructed the first apostles initially and then sent to them the third person of the Trinity, the Holy Ghost, who would guide them in the way of all truth.

Although it was disheartening to behold, I had to admit that the modern Catholic Church has produced practitioners who closely resemble their Protestant counterparts. Kenneth Jones's book, *Index of Leading Catholic Indicators*, tells a dismal story of the Church since Vatican II: most modern Catholics, for instance, no longer believe in the Real Presence of Christ in the Eucharist, and most do not understand the Mass as a sacrifice but rather as a shared and symbolic meal. Is it any wonder, then, that most no longer understand the voluntary missing of Mass to be a mortal sin? Indeed, most seem to have lost a sensitivity to sin in general, let alone to the distinction between mortal and venial sin; as a consequence, they have little use for the sacrament of confession. Many also seem to have forgotten Mary, the Mother of our Lord. Few pray to the saints and angels. And most simply do not bother to follow difficult Catholic teachings about such things as birth control. In short, many of the Catholic laity have become moral and theological relativists, adapting the Faith of the Ages to themselves, to what works for them in their own modern conception of reality, rather than conforming themselves to the real reality of Heaven.

This is the Church I found when I converted. This is the *Novus Ordo* (the new order) springing forth from post-conciliar Catholicism. For fourteen years I simply accepted the fact with a shrug. A disappointment? Certainly, but where else was I to go? In practice, I myself was no different than many of my fellow parishioners and much worse than some heroic others: I fulfilled my weekly Mass obligation, often leaving early, as soon as I had received the sacrament; I went only rarely to confession; I never sought the aid of saints or angels; I never said the Rosary; I moseyed about mostly unaware that I had chosen the vocational state of marriage years ago and therefore without any conscious acceptance of my duties or of the sacrifices associated with such state. Instead, I pursued my own artistic ends somewhat aimlessly and always with a certain sadness.

But I never thought about leaving the Church. I held on to the idea that, despite the malaise of its practitioners (and, I fear, many of its religious), the Church still contained the truth, still offered us the sacraments, the saints, the deposit of faith, all the things I had pondered before converting. In my efforts to make sense of it all, I held these things—these very Catholic things—apart in my mind and resigned myself to the notion that they existed separately from actual human experience, something like Platonic ideals. Then in 2003 I attended for the first time the Tridentine Mass, the Mass of Pope St. Pius V, the Mass of the Ages, virtually unchanged for nearly half a millennium.

Waking Up

My first exposure to the old Mass was in the beautiful river town of La Crosse, Wisconsin, where there was an Indult granted by then Bishop Raymond Burke. I had just moved my family to nearby Winona, Minnesota, in accepting a teaching post there. With me to my first traditional Mass, I took my eleven-year-old daughter, Kate. We awoke together as from a dream. There before our eyes, in the movements and postures of the priest and his assistants, in the ancient sounds of the Latin words and in the appeal of that one voice, a single ecclesiastical tongue, in the meaning of those prayers, the extensive adoration of the three persons of the Trinity, in the summoning of many saints and martyrs by name, in the hailing of our Lady, in the deeply reverent consecration, the priest with his back to us, his head lifted to the crucifix in front of him, the breaking of our Lord in the perfect sacrifice He offers in love to the Father, in virtually every nuance of this Mass was the Church I had gone looking for so many years ago. At last there was alignment: between the idea of Catholicism and its practice, between the Church I thought I was converting to and the one that now stood before me, between the virtues of hope and faith. The long haze of disillusionment cleared, and I knew for certain that the Church had indeed survived, a tough but delicate lily pushing her way impossibly through this present layer of snow.

If all traditional Catholicism had to offer was the Tridentine Mass, it would be enough, I think, because the Mass, by its very nature, is catechetical. The liturgy teaches even as it orients; the emphasis is always vertical; the treasures of the Church are constantly reiterated in plain view of the faithful. The Mass, as the grounding point of contact among the members of the Church, contains all the marks of that Church: it is catholic in the sense that it is universal (the same everywhere, made even more so by the exclusive use of Latin); it is holy in the sense that it directs our attention perpetually to all that is above us in the heavenly hierarchy; it is apostolic in the way that it came into being, beginning with the Canon—the core words instituted by our Lord—and developing within the apostolic tradition; and it makes us one in Holy Communion, which is, of course, the only way possible for true unity to occur. Any other claim to unity among Christians resides in the natural realm, is a group of humans holding beliefs more or less loosely in common as they would in a political party or an enthusiasts' club. But the unity of Christ's Church is more akin to the blood that binds an extended human family. God gives of His incarnated Self to us, and by way of His Blood, which we take into our own bodies, we are quite literally of one family. In fact, because it is Christ and no other who unites us both materially and spiritually, we become more deeply bonded in this heavenly family than we could ever be in our earthly families, which are but an intimation of the other.

I digress with this consideration of unity because it gets at the heart of the difference between the *Novus Ordo* churches I attended for fourteen years and the traditional churches I have attended since. The *Novus Ordo* church, like the Protestant churches, has attempted to build unity with human hands by trying to make the Church more appealing, more "relevant" to modern man. The damage is done deftly by a few sleights of hand: In the

Mass, change the language to the vernacular despite the inherent risk of disunity by way of inevitable translation discrepancies; reduce the number and elegant formality of prayers; reduce references to the saints and to Mary (almost as if these ancient lights are a kind of superstitious embarrassment to the "modern" Catholic mind); involve lay persons in the liturgy; involve lay persons in the distribution of the Sacrament; de-emphasize the sacrificial nature of the Eucharist by putting the priest on the other side of the altar, inviting the image of his presiding at the family table; de-emphasize the material presence of Christ in the host by encouraging (and sometimes forcing) the faithful to receive Him in a standing position and in the palms of their hands; encourage popular, culturally relevant music that operates almost exclusively on a simplistic and emotional level; preach sermons that are invariably bland so as not to run the risk of offending anyone. Stop speaking of the need for increased prayer and voluntary penance, of the need for frequent confession, of the need to utterly amend one's life. Virtually every distinguishing characteristic of the *Novus Ordo* church is one of accommodation to the spirit of the age. Yes, Christ is still present in the Eucharist, but when every aspect of Catholic life and liturgy has been revised to emphasize and accommodate the whims of culture, then individual Catholic souls are at great risk. Through the fog of themselves and their fellow parishioners, the view of Christ is obscured. Our will, damaged already by the fall, is further weakened and requires heroic exertion for priest and faithful alike to cooperate with the grace that is offered. And although there are notable exceptions, most are not heroic. Most are confused and floundering, lost sheep, united more to each other than to their Shepherd.

By contrast, the Tridentine Mass seeks not to make the faithful more comfortable nor to involve them more in a false sense of spiritual egalitarianism. Rather the traditional Mass, by its every word and rubric, strives to reveal and exalt the only possible means of true Christian unity: Christ Himself. This oneness is timeless, not in the least subject to the errors of Modernity–basically, the elevation of the individuality of self–or any other heresy for that matter. It is the visible manifestation of what Christ intimated when He said to Peter, "Upon this rock I will build my Church, and the gates of hell shall not prevail against it."

This solidity in the traditional Mass seems to carry over to its priests as well. In the years since my family and I started attending, we have received more consistent and unequivocal Catholic instruction, grounded deeply in the deposit of faith, than in all our previous Catholic years combined. I have now a clearer understanding of the last five hundred years of ideas and how they have affected both the Church and modern man. In the depths of traditional Catholic faith, I am finding an articulation not just for what I have experienced in modern Christianity over the years but also for the whole of my life. I perceive the context for my most important choices along the way, the errors in some of my most cherished philosophies, the tepidity in my religious life, the aimlessness of my artistic life. We cannot see how we are infused with the spirit of the world until we step outside the world we are in. We step outside the world we are in by way of something that stands apart from such a world. The Church, instituted by Christ and guided by the Holy Ghost for nearly two thousand years, ought to be that timeless and lucid entity by which we can see. For me it finally is.

For as long as I can remember, a part of me has been trying to wake up from the dream of myself and shake my head in the clear, brisk air of the real world. Although I have slept late and my eyes are still adjusting to the light, I know now who it was that woke me up. At the moment of consecration during every Mass where we assist, when the priest is holding up the Body of our dear Lord about to be broken, the chapel bells ring out across the beautiful bluffs that rise above the Mississippi River. That they should sound at such a moment is an anomaly in the modern age. With clarity of tone and timeless beckoning, they send an urgent message into the sleeping valley of the world: Something is happening here, something of indescribable importance. It is an ancient melody that most of us have all but forgotten. These bells are full of yearning. They sing the most poignant song that has ever been sung.

> This essay first appeared in the May 2007 issue of the *New Oxford Review*, 1069 Kains Avenue, Berkeley, CA 94706, U.S.A., and is reprinted with permission. Michael Larson teaches English at Minnesota State College–Southeast Technical. His collection of poetry, *What We Wish We Knew*, was published in 2005, and his poems, stories, and essays have appeared in a variety of periodicals. He lives with his wife and three children in Winona, Minnesota, where they attend Mass at the chapel of the North American Seminary for the Society of St. Pius X.

Mary Ann Kreitzer

Weathering the Storm: A Catholic's Journey from Chaos to Hope

It was late August 1964. The bishops were preparing to meet in September for the third session of Vatican II. The Council had approved the documents on the liturgy the previous year and the first vernacular Mass in the United States would be celebrated at the Twenty-fifth Annual Liturgical Week Conference late in the month. The liturgists decided at that meeting that the translation needed work, but their flawed version had to suffice since expansion to the entire U.S. Church was slated for November and they were eager for the novelty. Few parishioners in the pew had any idea that their Church was about to be swept by changes that would alter not only the liturgical foundations of their worship, but the moral landscape of the world.

I certainly did not. A cradle Catholic from a large military family and a recent graduate from a girls' Catholic academy in Pennsylvania, I was only concerned about one change—leaving home for the first time to start an exciting new adventure at Trinity College in Washington, D.C. I was a devout teenager who rose early during Lent to attend 6:30 A.M. Mass with my mother before school; I belonged to the Sodality and had a particular devotion to the Blessed Mother and St. Ann, for whom I was named; and my deep faith, indeed unshakable I thought, was anchored securely to the rock of Peter. The hurricane that would inundate the Church in the United States would wash many off the solid rock and into a sea of confusion and chaos, however, as for a time it would me.

Love in the Ruins

My years at Trinity were nonetheless in many ways a normal college experience with classes, a part-time campus job, exams, activities, friendships, dating, and coping a little with homesickness. My chief focus was the responsibilities of the day, which usually meant hunkering down in the stacks of the library basement studying for the next test, midterm finals, or passing Metaphysics; and I spent little time reflecting on where some of this education was taking me or whether the messages being transmitted were truly Catholic since I thought all that a given. After all, my mother attended Trinity before me, class of '39, and she often spoke of its exemplary Catholic education, the devout reverence of the priests and nuns, and her excellent apologetics training. I accordingly trusted the nuns and other professors at Trinity, though the experience my mother had known was gone.

Senior year I found myself down the street at nearby Catholic University mingling with hundreds of students rallying to support a priest named Charlie Curran, who'd been denied tenure for his perverted views on human sexuality. My roommate and I drifted in the crowd as observers, there not out of conviction, but out of (clueless) curiosity. I wasn't impressed by Curran's speech; I was simply baffled. What did the Church stand for? How could a priest shake his fist at the pope? And if he could, who couldn't? When the university caved in to the student theater, it was a huge boat-swamping wave for me personally, though even then I did not grasp its importance; I only knew that Curran had "won." Exactly what I and my generation had lost I would only come to understand over time as further perversion and heresy assaulted the Church again and again.

There were many comparable events during my Trinity years. As a sophomore I took the required moral theology course, which did little more than extol (im)moral relativism. Students were indoctrinated with the trite ideas of Joseph Fletcher's "situational ethics," with Harvey Cox's undergirding of "liberation" theology, and with a whole panoply of Freudian and/or Marxian psychological theory with no relation to reality except being the latest effort to escape from reality. Ironically, since so many of our parents had taught us to respect authority, with particular deference to priests and nuns, it was not so hard to swallow the same poison of betrayal the clerics had.

One final example of all this was a "retreat" at Trinity for young women with Fr. James Kavanaugh, author of *A Modern Priest Looks at His Outdated Church*. Kavanaugh was funny in a cynical sort of way as he ridiculed Church teachings and told students if they didn't get anything out of Mass they shouldn't bother going. He rejoiced at all the changes after Vatican II, seeing them as just a beginning, anticipating women's ordination and an end to priestly celibacy with glee, but providing no wisdom against, in fact not so subtly supporting, the mantras of drugs, sex, and immorality that characterized the '60's.[1] And, of course, he was particularly excited by the elimination of the Latin Mass.

In short, like so many in those days, I entered college a Catholic and upon leaving it four years later also left the Church. The vast clerical apostasy that decimated the priesthood would necessarily demand rejection of the ancient liturgy. And though these clerics no doubt knew and welcomed the devastating impact the change would have (and did have) on the lay faithful, it can hardly be argued the change itself is what provoked the false clerics, since all of them had been nurtured on the ancient rite. So there must have been a deeper problem, of faith itself, also of wisdom. Yet is there any question that, once our shepherds respond to the grace of these same virtues, they will again embrace the reverent traditional Mass, and for much the same reasons the apostates rejected it?

It is, perhaps, not surprising that, as my faith unraveled, the changes in the Mass did not seem so important to me. Yet con-

---

[1] In the early 1990's, Fr. Kavanaugh drifted into my life again via a book given to my daughter by the chaplain of the Newman Club at the University of Virginia. No longer "Father," Mr. Kavanaugh had married, divorced, and at that time authored silly poetry about being on a journey with no destination. Its drivel was a too perfect template for so much of Church governance since my student days, but in using it to attack the faith of my daughter, the UVA Newman Club priest showed how poisoned so much of the priesthood still was, and is; and how determined they still were, and are, to poison others.

sider how much has been lost: the mystery of a deeper and richer world to which the Latin carried the worshipper, the accompanying reverence and joy that goes with it, the beautiful Gregorian chant and sacred polyphony—now replaced by the mood of a Rotary Club social with almost comically inane hymns, including openly heretical ones. And what is the point of eliminating the altar rails and receiving the Lord of the universe by hand, if not to undermine faith in His transubstantial Presence? What better way to accomplish this than by eliminating, along with all real music, the reverent beauty of silence? Or as Screwtape put it in one of his letters to his nephew Wormwood:

> Music and silence—how I detest them both! How thankful we should be that ever since our Father entered Hell…no square inch of infernal space and no moment of infernal time has been surrendered to either of those abominable forces, but all has been occupied by Noise—Noise, the grand dynamism, the audible expression of all that is exultant, ruthless, and virile—Noise which alone defends us from silly qualms, despairing scruples, and impossible desires. We will make the whole universe a noise in the end.[2]

Within two years of graduation I had married, was a mother, and by God's grace had returned to the Faith; but to a Church that seemed much different from the one I had known growing up. My husband and I wanted to build a family centered on Christ, through the Church, but seeking opportunities to do that often revealed overt hostility to both. For one horrendous example, on being asked to teach CCD to teenagers, we were expected to use a textbook from a series that included a six-week session on the Black Mass and the occult and another that didn't even mention Jesus' name until the last page of the book, after Zorba the Greek. Indeed, everywhere we turned there were strange and visibly evil ideas being promoted, especially to the young. Our objections were indulged and sometimes resolved, but always we were confronted with new horrors.

---

[2] C. S. Lewis, *The Screwtape Letters* (New York: MacMillan Paperbacks, 1977), pp. 102-3.

Mary Ann Kreitzer

I am ashamed and embarrassed to confess my own liturgical participation in some of the worst of them, and today I marvel at how I, how so many, could have been so docile before the persistent and organized desecration of the most sacred expression of the Faith itself, the Mass.

In my own case it was via the ecumenical Christian Family Movement (CFM), which was more or less modeled after the "base communities" by which "liberation theology" was promoted in Latin America. Some five or six couples would gather, in my experience always Catholics, along with our chaplains, priests and seminarians from the Franciscan Order of Friars Minor. Our meetings often began with a noisy guitar and tambourine hootenanny home Mass with one of the priests presiding.

In the egalitarian style of the day we called them Joe or Kevin or Phil or Steve, rarely Father. These "liturgies" were frequently said without benefit of vestments except for a stole, and they commonly violated many of the rubrics of the Mass. On one occasion at a CFM family retreat, Joe (a Jesuit this time) had each married couple invest each other with stoles, the "sign of our priesthood to each other," and restate our marriage vows. A strange concept to me now, it was one more example of denigrating the genuine priestly charism of the ordained while instilling a false sense of clericalism in the laity. It fit with the times when priests were encouraged to escape the sanctuary while the laity flocked to it.

Most of our chaplains, regardless of their order (we also had a Paulist for a time) reflected the confusion and even mendacity among so many religious after Vatican II. Among the Franciscans, several defended contraception, another admired Charlie Curran and his perverted theology, one seminarian (who later headed the Catholic Theological Society of America) held and justified the same viciously pro-abortion advocacy of Jesuit Fr. Robert Drinan, a revelation that made me literally sick. His defense of the indefensible disturbed others in the group as well, although, I'm sad to say, not all.

One of the worst abuses during those two decades with CFM, and I hate to speak of it now, was our common practice of making

Love in the Ruins

Communion bread for home Masses. Whether the recipe originated with one of our chaplains, or I think more likely one of our lay members, I can't recall; but it included eggs, honey, and oil, making it invalid matter for the Consecration. Shockingly, all of the priests condoned it and never refused its use for Mass. Perhaps it was best Our Blessed Lord didn't have strictly to be present while we stood for the Consecration, circled the room, hugging, laughing, and chatting away during the sign of peace, and circled the "altar" holding hands at the Our Father. Whether or not real or valid wine was used I can't for certain say (we always received under both species), but given the abuse, perhaps better had it no more been His Blood than it was His Body.

How deliberate was the CFM assault on the faith of Catholics? Such operations among nuns, priestly orders, seminaries, the catechetical establishment, indeed everywhere, were ubiquitous; but in CFM's case its founders, Pat and Patty Crowley, were admitted devotees of the atheist community organizer Saul Alinsky, who dedicated his famous book, *Rules for Radicals*–I'm not kidding–to Satan. The Crowleys were also on the papal birth control commission that told Pope Paul VI that the Church should approve and promote contraception, and indeed the Crowleys, particularly Patty, were outraged when, with *Humanae Vitae,* His Holiness did the obvious by reaffirming constant Church teaching instead. At a CFM convention in the 1970's, Patty, by then a widow, actively lobbied against a resolution condemning abortion, which passed nonetheless because she had lost control of the CFM leadership, and the fundamental good sense of Catholic parents was coming to the fore. At her death Patty was eulogized by the excommunicated anti-Catholic group known as Call to Action for being their "godmother."

So the attack on the faith, at least by the Crowleys and their allies, was intentional and organized; and CFM, like many other institutions, appears to have been designed to dilute the faith through the stress on ecumenism, protestantizing the liturgy, and attacking the ministerial priesthood. Like myself, Mrs. Crowley was an alumna of Trinity College, to which she credited some insipid class on social justice with opening her "mind," though apparently her brains fell out in the process. Pro-abortion fanatics Congressional House Speaker Nancy Pelosi and Kansas Governor Kathleen Sebelius, incidentally, are two other products of Trinity's (anti)Catholic education.

Nonetheless, despite the damage such groups as CFM did and were apparently designed to do by their founders, their efforts to undermine the genuinely Catholic element they recruited sometimes backfired. As so often happens, what was intended for evil, God used for good. So it proved for me in that it was through our local CFM group that we hosted a lecture–before *Roe v. Wade*–featuring pro-life pioneers Jack and Barbara Willke, who spoke to over eight hundred about the reality of abortion. Though my husband and I were already naturally pro-life, that lecture proved a decisive turning point. We soon offered a shelter home to unwed mothers and continued to do so for many in the decades that followed, but also became deeply involved in lobbying, picketing, sidewalk counseling, working at a pregnancy counseling center and, in the late 1970's, I also participated in some of the earliest rescues ever done at the abortion mills.

In fact, my involvement with rescue re-opened my eyes to what we had also lost with the changes in the Mass. That did not come, however, until 1992 with a major Spring of Life campaign of rescues in Buffalo, New York. Partly this was due to spending twenty-four days in jail with 150 other women, several of whom were traditional and astute, and with whom serious discussion revealed to me how dependent the abortion holocaust had become on corruption of the clerical establishment in the Catholic Church.

I particularly recall a discussion about Communion in the hand, the real purpose behind it, its promotion by materially apostate clerics, and the episcopal support for this attack on reverence and belief in our Lord's Real Presence in the Eucharist. We were sitting on the floor in a prison hallway where dozens of us slept, only a few inches separating our individual mattresses. Their explanation and the attendant discussion brought home how much the irreverence and so many abuses at Mass were not just individual flukes, but something very much like a systematic program. And suddenly, I understood. I knew. I'd been there and done it.

When a local priest came to say Mass for us in the prison, I knelt on the hard concrete floor and, for the first time in two decades, received Communion from this *alter Christus* on my tongue; and that simple gesture touched my soul near its core; it made me long for a return to the altar rail and the reverence I had known in my youth.

The time in prison thus became, as well as a witness, a retreat. In those long days devoting hours to saying the rosary, reading the Bible, and praying, I pondered the relationship between the desecration of children on the altar of abortion and the desecration at the altar of God. A reigning Babel had built its tower of deceit, had sought to destroy our faith, and if that failed, then our children's.

How obvious it all ultimately was: the false teachings, the mockery, the open honoring of the Faith's enemies at church functions while persecuting those who objected, and doing it in so many ways—even, I recalled, to the ridiculous and almost possessed point of forbidding the devout to pray the rosary publicly after daily Mass, or to genuflect before receiving Communion. And there was the appalling cowardice, even from presumably believing bishops, who did so little to defend the flock—and, of course, the immorality, though I had no idea how vicious and demonic it was, preying on children: the abortion ethic, so to speak, carried to the larger population. How had it happened, I wondered? That it had, and that it was organized was clear enough, but how had it gotten to that point, and seemingly overnight? How could such manifest and open enemies of the Catholic Faith come to be in charge of so many of her institutions?

My determination to resist solidified, grew, and was finally given form in 1995 when a brazenly heretical group invaded the Arlington diocese to organize in our parishes. Known as "Call to Action," (CTA) its members openly mocked the priesthood and the Faith, advertising men who'd abandoned their vows but who for a fee, through "Rent-a-priest," were ready to simulate them at weddings and funerals and such. They promoted another group as well called "Promises," a group for women having affairs with active priests. When the bishop refused to ban this outrageously heretical group from church property, I joined with friends who'd decided that, since the bishop wouldn't defend the faithful, it was time for us to defend ourselves.

At CTA's second parish organizational meeting–at Christ the Redeemer in Sterling, Virginia–about a hundred Catholics showed up to confront the assault. Because a handful had disrupted their previous meeting, the CTA organizers brought in the police this time and, confident this intimidation would smother any protest, they mockingly welcomed us. They failed, however, to recognize that they were also dealing with veterans of the rescue movement who were not afraid of the threat of arrest, nor of its reality.

As the meeting heated up, a CTA operative and public advocate of adultery, who was on his second wife at the time but would go on to a third before long, began pointing out people to arrest. Police ultimately dragged out and cited eight Catholics, some of us publicly reciting the rosary during the travesty, provoking much local attention and the dismay of the chancery. Soon after this, a memo from the chancellor went to all the diocese's pastors:

> In response to repeated recommendations made by a number of priests during our Presbyteral Meeting on March 29th, we are making explicit what is already implicit in Canon Law: that pastors and other administrators of the church properties are not to allow use of their facilities to groups who advocate against church teachings or legitimate church practices.[3]

This victory gave birth nine months later to a group, under the patronage of St. Joan of Arc, called *Les Femmes:* The Women of Truth, dedicated to fighting for the Faith against its enemies, and beyond that for authentic Catholic culture. We also sought to encourage faithful Catholics weary over liturgical abuses and scandals plaguing the diocese, for as a priest adviser told us, "If

---

[3] Fr. Robert Rippy, Memorandum to all pastors and administrators of church properties, April 3, 1995.

you can't stop a scandal, the next best thing is to shine light on it."

In my own parish, Mass was comparatively reverent. Our pastor had restored the bells, the *Kyrie*, the *Sanctus*, and the *Agnus Dei*; one priest even wore black vestments for funerals and on All Souls' Day. The congregation often heard solid sermons addressing abortion and contraception, a rarity in this diocese as in others. Even so, I was often forced to close my eyes from showmen strutting on the altar, and with many others I longed for the priest to turn *ad orientem* again. At these times I reflected how wise the Church once had been to insist the priest join the people in turning towards God instead of towards each other.

I was fortunate in being able to attend daily Mass at a nearby Poor Clare Monastery within the parish bounds, where liturgical aberrations had made no inroads; Mother Abbess wouldn't tolerate it. In addition, as the priest faced the Sisters on the other side of the grill, I could again see the body posture of the ancient rite as Father raised the sacred species over his head; and I joined the Apostle St. Thomas with the eternal prayer of faith, and penance, and gratitude: "My Lord and my God. My Jesus, Mercy." In 2003 I was able to attend an intense and transformative five-day Ignatian retreat, and its Masses were all in the ancient Latin rite. Retreatants traveled to the Washington Archdiocese because the Tridentine was still (illegally, if I've read Pope Benedict's motu proprio right) not allowed in Arlington. So I packed my old dog-eared Roman Missal, the faithful Mass companion of my childhood, though I had not looked at it in years. When I opened it for daily Mass on the first morning of the retreat, I found the inscription "To Mary Ann...Love, Mother and Dad" in my deceased mother's handwriting.

Kneeling in the pew, I wept, of course, wept at the depth and wonder of my parents' love for me, and God's, and of His choice to reveal it again at this moment, so tenderly. You can imagine my joy at using that missal again, with its broken spine and shabby ribbons, reading the prayers of St. Ambrose and Aquinas in preparation for Mass, and understanding why they called it the Mass of Angels. Their Mass, and that of so many saints, but also so many suffering, sinful, repentant, and, indeed, holy Catholic men and women throughout the ages, from all the ends of the earth. I was again united to them all across time: to St. Augustine and St. Bernard and St. Thomas More, to the Irish on the hills and the Pole in the gulag, to St. Teresa of Avila and St. Dominic and St. Joan of Arc, to the obscure Aztec freed of his demons, the simple Filipina housewife, the Curé of Ars and Padre Pio, to all the nuns and monks and workers and thinkers, to St. Therese of Lisieux and St. Juan Diego, and millions, indeed billions of men and women from everywhere, who had knelt with a quickening of the soul, as mine now did, to hear the priest proclaim: "*In nomine Patris, et Filii, et Spiritus Sancti.*" As Father bowed and said the prayers at the foot of the altar, I realized once more how much was lost, indeed destroyed. The ancient liturgy recognized both the profound joy of worship—"I will go in unto the altar of God, the God who gives joy to my youth"—as it did the need for the sinner to prepare his heart for it: "Take away from us our iniquities, we beseech thee, O Lord: that we may be worthy to enter with pure minds into the Holy of Holies." There were no altar boys during the retreat, so we responded from the pews, and though I had not heard the Latin for years, all was familiar, all was warm, all was from God who'd given joy to my youth.

Five years have passed since then, and the struggle continues, as it will in this vale of tears, though it's a vale of glory, too. That my own faith survived is to me a mystery of the kind God seems unwilling to reveal about faith and its nurturing. Perhaps the even greater mystery is of love and of prayer; for I can't help but feel, and even know, that the prayers of my parents in this world and from the next, and those of Our Lady, have kept me from straying very far from the Faith's foundations. Through much foolishness, and sin too, my love for our Lord in the Eucharist, and for His Blessed Mother, remained my lifeline. From them also came my love for the least of His brethren: the assaulted, the defenseless, and the innocent unborn.

Love in the Ruins

Now, with His Holiness Pope Benedict's announcement that, despite all the fury and determination to destroy it, the Mass of the ages was never suppressed, never illegal, was with us always, and always will be, there seems cause for no little hope, even in our lifetime. The manifest nonsense and horror of the present hour will soon spend itself, does so even as I write. From out of its chaos and rubble can we not already see that the ancient Mass provides the light by which the Church shall not only rise herself, but restore some measure of sanity to the world? Surely so, for the light is rising in the east, and God has visited His people as they come again to worship His Son, Who taketh away the sins of the world, and our sins, too.

> Mary Ann Kreitzer is a founder and the president of Les Femmes (www.lesfemmes-thetruth.org), a Catholic group dedicated to defending the faith and authentic Catholic Culture, and of the Catholic Media Coalition (www.catholicmediacoalition.org). She lives in Woodstock, Virginia.

John Vennari

A Front-Row Seat to the Revolution

Pope Pius XII died on October 9, 1958. I was barely six months old at the time. My infancy and toddler years coincided with the reign of Pope John XXIII. Consequently, I did not grow up in the Church of the 1950's. My experience of pre-Vatican II practice was limited to the immediate years prior to transitions wrought by the Council.

Because I attended Catholic grade school, I had a front row seat to the Conciliar revolution that swept the Church throughout the 1960's. When I was in first grade, I was learning the *Kyrie*. By the time I got to fourth grade, I was learning *Kumbaya*. When I was in first grade, all we saw of Sister Joan Labouré was her hands and her face. By the time I got to eighth grade, I knew that Sister Kevin Leonard had red hair and varicose veins.

I thus had a front row seat to all the change going at the time: a change in appearance, in attitude, in liturgical practice, in doctrine.

Part of this change included the massive renovations of the interior of my parish church. St. Leo's in Northeast Philadelphia was magnificent inside and out. I can only describe the interior as a kind of mini-cathedral: a soaring Gothic high altar with matching side altars, beautiful statues, holy wall murals, a mighty octagon-shaped pulpit ornamented with carved cherub heads, black and white tile floor, handsome communion rail.

As a little boy, every time I walked into that church, I knew it was God's house. This was not only because of the splendid interior that catapulted the mind and heart to heaven. It was also because of the attitude of reverence typical of Catholics in the early 1960's.

There was absolutely no talking in church. Parishioners wore their Sunday best for Mass. Women dressed modestly; and I am not talking about frumpy denim jumpers, but fine dresses, hats and veils. The vast majority of men wore suits, or jackets and ties. Attending Mass in sneakers was unthinkable. All reverence was given to Our Lord in the Blessed Sacrament in the tabernacle, and this deference dictated every aspect of our dress and comportment while in church.

This was a time of high attendance at Mass, at both the upstairs church and downstairs chapel. There were many Masses each Sunday starting at 6:00 A.M. going to 12:15 P.M. The latest Mass, the 12:15, was a Traditional High Mass packed to the rafters each week.

In 1964, just as the Council was winding down, our parish was assigned a new pastor. He stayed for four years and completely renovated—that is, *wreckovated*—the interior of St. Leo's. The Gothic high altar was torn down to be replaced with an oak *Novus Ordo* table so the priest could face the people. Out went the communion rail, the pulpit, most of the statues. The tile floor was covered with red carpet; the beautiful murals ripped off the wall and replaced with new plaster and blue paint. By 1968, the newly renovated interior was barren and desolate; a fitting vessel for a new liturgy with the same characteristics soon to come.

Silliness and Shenanigans

In 1969, two events occurred: one of world-wide significance and one of personal significance. Of world-wide significance, the New Mass came on to the scene; of personal significance, I started to play guitar.

As soon as I began to play guitar, I joined the newly formed "Guitar Mass." I could do this as a rank beginner because in order to be in the guitar Mass, one did not have to be any good. Anyone who could get through the standard C-Am-F-G7 chord changes of the 1950's had all the talent it required. The music was about as challenging as a kazoo.

In time, I quit the guitar Mass. Also, as time passed, I became increasingly uneasy with the silliness and the shenanigans I saw presented to me as Sunday Mass. I came from a good Catholic family, but it was not at this time a traditionalist family. I had no access to traditionalist literature and did not know there was any movement fighting for the old Liturgy.

I became disillusioned with the New Mass for two reasons: first, because of silliness. Second, because of shenanigans. As I sat Sunday after Sunday watching the Mass, it was obvious that the new rite was clumsy, awkward, and vapid. The New Mass brought with it the disappearance of reverence in church. Before and after Mass, people began to talk out loud to one another. The people's dress devolved from casual to slovenly and immodest. A man-centered spirit took over, and the parish church no longer breathed the atmosphere of God's house. Church attendance began to plummet.

I also remember something that left a deep impression on me. In order to get people involved in the liturgy–the so called "lay participation" of post-Vatican II rage–parishes began to set up the water and wine for Mass on a little table just outside the sanctuary near the pews so that lay people could bring the gifts to the priest at the Offertory. I noticed that all the pews around this water and wine table were always empty. This was true no matter which parish I attended. Another local parish set the table half way down the center aisle, which resulted in a swath of empty seats on both sides of the little table. People in general did not want to be involved in the new gimmick.

Then during the Offertory, there would always be that awkward moment when the priest would stand in front of the altar-table just *waiting* for someone to bring up the gifts. Finally, a mother in the congregation would nudge her son, and the two of them would saunter up to the priest carrying the water and wine, usually in slovenly attire: the mother in shorts, the boy in a Led Zepplin t-shirt. It was pointless, phony, ludicrous.

There was also the "kiss of peace," that twenty-seven seconds of forced friendliness just prior to reception of Communion. I did not understand the purpose of this childish practice, though I did question the sanity of whoever first introduced it and of those who welcomed its introduction.

I did not know much Catholic doctrine at the time, but by the grace of God, I had some sort of Catholic instinct that told me Mass should be reverent, awe-inspiring, godlike. The New Mass fit none of that criteria. Somehow I knew that a Catholic should not find his central act of worship as embarrassing as an amateur talent-show.

Nonetheless, I went to Mass each Sunday for one reason: If I deliberately missed Sunday Mass, I'd commit a mortal sin. If I'd die in a state of mortal sin, I'd go to hell forever. It's not worth it, I figured, I'll go to Mass.

Knowledge of mortal sin and fear of hellfire kept me on track during my adolescent years. Oddly enough, this consciousness of mortal sin told me there was something very wrong going on within the Church; something that went beyond silly liturgies.

I spent from autumn 1972 to spring 1976 in Catholic high school, where I was surrounded by a teaching order of priests and Brothers. Sin was practically never mentioned. I don't remember hearing the term "mortal sin" during my entire four years of high school. Usually, the only time a priest would mention sin would be to deny it. I knew, for example, that most sins against the Sixth and Ninth Commandments were mortal sins that send souls to hell, but we were told by certain priests, however, that these things were not sins anymore. Even a high-school couple could behave as if they were man and wife, said at least two priests at my Philadelphia high school, providing they loved one another.

In any case, my experience in Catholic high school told me there was something terribly out of order within the Church. Thankfully, my parents had a small selection of fine Catholic books around the house. I always read and believed these pre-Vatican II books rather than my modern teachers because the older books tallied with common sense. This, incidentally, is one of the main reasons I am committed to the Catholic Press. I know the great good of which true Catholic literature is capable. I really learned my faith once I got out of school. In fact, if I had to rely on what I learned at my Catholic school, I would have lost my faith a long time ago.

It was in late 1977 that I learned for the first time that the New Mass was written with the help of six Protestant ministers and that the changes in this New Mass were a mirror image of the liturgical changes enacted by the leaders of the sixteenth-century Protestant revolt. I remember back then wondering: if imitation is the sincerest form of flattery, why are our Church leaders imitating men who have rejected bedrock tenets of the Catholic Faith? I further learned the *Novus Ordo Missae* was written to satisfy the demands of ecumenism. It finally all made sense. The New Mass did not *seem* quite Catholic because, in fact, it was *not* quite Catholic.

I wanted the old Latin Mass, as it was clear the New Mass was not a lamb without blemish, but the sacrifice of Cain in Calvinist robes. I learned the old Mass was still celebrated in various places, but had trouble getting to it. I was a full-time musician working until 2:00 A.M. in night clubs (during the "Disco" era) and often did not get home until 4:00. Also, I spent much of 1979 on the road. As a result, I did not finally attend my first Tridentine Mass until early 1980. Around this time, I quit the music world as I became increasingly aware of the disordered nature of pop music and joined an establishment that was attempting to be a traditional Benedictine monastery. I was there for a number of years, though I never took final vows.

Since 1980, I have attended the Latin Tridentine Mass exclusively; the reason goes beyond the banalities of the New Mass mentioned earlier. I never attend the New Mass because I believe it to be a liturgy for a new religion: the new religion of ecumenism. Ecumenism was the guiding principle–the *formative principle*–of the New Mass. And modern ecumenism is a non-Catholic principle always condemned by the Church[1] because it places the one true religion established by Jesus Christ on the same level as false creeds and because it serves to perpetuate the state of separation of those outside the Church, rather than bring them into it. St. Maximilian Kolbe, well aware of these facts, said clearly in 1933, "Ecumenism is the enemy of the Immaculata."[2]

The ecumenical and Protestant direction of Vatican II's liturgical reform was evident early on, even during the Council itself. The Anglican John Moorman, D.D., a Protestant observer at the Council, noted in 1963, "In reading the Schema on the Liturgy, I could not help thinking that if the Church of Rome were to carry out all the reforms they proposed they would one day find that they had triumphantly invented the Book of Common Prayer." Moorman listed five propositions made by the Council on which he positively commented: 1) "The plan for more and varied use in Scripture"; 2) "The Place of the Laity in the Worship of the Church" (urging laity to have a 'part to play' in liturgy); 3) "The Use of the Vernacular"; 4) "The need for more preaching"; 5) "Communion under Both Kinds." Moorman saw these proposals as of "particular interest to the non-Roman Catholic world and to have special significance in the cause of Christian Unity."[3]

The reader is struck by the fact that all of these proposals shift the focus away from the central aspect of sacrifice to a Protestant approach. This is precisely what the *Novus Ordo* achieved. It was not constructed to be a clear expression of the Catholic Faith, nor was it designed for the proper worship of God that is His due. It was formulated, rather, as surrender to Protestantism for the sake of the new ecumenism.

Archbishop Annibale Bugnini, the architect of the New Mass, admitted this openly: "We must strip from our Catholic

---

[1] See for example Pope Pius XI's 1928 Encyclical *Mortalium Animos*, "On Fostering True Christian Unity."
[2] Entry of Diary dated April 23, 1933. Cited from *The Immaculata Our Ideal* by Fr. Karl Stehlin (Warsaw: Te Deum, 2005), p. 37.
[3] John Moorman, "An Observer Looks at the Schema on the Liturgy," *Vatican II: The Theological Dimension* (A full year of *The Thomist*, 1963, published in book form), The Thomist Press, 1963, pp. 440-50.

prayers and from the Catholic liturgy everything which can be the shadow of a stumbling block for our separated brethren; that is, for the Protestants."[4]

Likewise, journalist Jean Guitton, a close friend and confidant of Pope Paul VI, confirmed that it was the direct aim of the Pope to protestantize the liturgy. In a radio interview in the 1990's, Guitton said:

> The intention of Paul VI with regard to what is commonly called the Mass, was to reform the Catholic liturgy in such a way that it should almost coincide with the Protestant liturgy–but what is curious is that Paul VI did that to get as close as possible to the Protestant Lord's supper...there was with Paul VI an ecumenical intention to remove, or at least to correct, or at least to relax, what was too Catholic, in the traditional sense, in the Mass and, I repeat, to get the Catholic Mass closer to the Calvinist Mass.[5]

New Mass, New Religion

The stance of many Catholics in regard to the New Mass often revolves around the question of validity.

If the consecration of the bread and wine at the New Mass is valid, goes the reasoning, then the Catholic must accept it and have no objection.

I believe this to be an incorrect approach. The reason I never attend the New Mass has nothing to do with validity. Rather, it is because the New Mass is the fruit of the new ecumenical belief system. One of the main tenets of this system is the "new ecclesiology," the false belief that the Church of Christ is actually bigger than the Catholic Church. Vatican II propounded this doctrine, particularly in *Lumen Gentium* 8 where we read, "the Church of Christ subsists in the Catholic Church." The Council Fathers refused to say what the Catholic Church has always taught, that the Church of Christ *exists exclusively in* the Catholic Church. Pope Pius XII pronounced this doctrine twice within the short span of seven years. In the 1943 encyclical *Mystici Corporis*, Pope Pius

---

[4] *L'Osservatore Romano*, March 19, 1965.
[5] Quoted from Michael McGrade, "Redemptionis Sacramentum, DOA, RIP," *Christian Order*, August/September, 2004.

XII taught "the true Church of Jesus Christ...is the One, Holy, Catholic, Apostolic Roman Church."[6] This clearly means that the Church of Christ is not composed of the Catholic Church and other "Christian" denominations.

Pope Pius XII reiterated this doctrine in his 1950 encyclical *Humani Generis*: "The Mystical Body of Christ and the Roman Catholic Church are one and the same thing." In the same paragraph, Pius complained of those who "reduce to a meaningless formula the necessity of belonging to the true Church in order to gain eternal salvation."[7]

Vatican II's new definition implies, however, that the Church of Christ is actually bigger than the Catholic Church and somehow includes other denominations. The progressivist Fr. Edward Schillebeeckx, O.P., who exercised considerable influence over the direction of the Council, gets right to the heart of this new definition. He wrote, "At Vatican Council II the Roman Catholic Church officially abandoned its monopoly over the Christian religion."[8]

If anyone wishes to dismiss Schillebeeckx as too radical, similar statements can be quoted from the Jesuit Avery Dulles, who was created a cardinal by Pope John Paul II in 2001. Dulles wrote:

> *The Church of Jesus Christ is not exclusively identical to the Roman Catholic Church.* It does indeed subsist in Roman Catholicism, but it is also present in varying modes and degrees in other Christian communities to the extent that they too are what God initiated in Jesus and are obedient to the inspirations of Christ's Spirit. As a result of their common sharing in the reality of the one Church, the several Christian communities already have with one another a real but imperfect communion.[9]

On March 24, 1998, Vatican Secretary of State Cardinal Sodano gave a speech in which he praised the infamous Hans

---

[6] *Mystici Corporis*, N.C.W.C. edition, 1943, §13, p. 8.
[7] *Humani Generis*, N.C.W.C. edition, 1950, §27, p. 12.
[8] E. Schillebeeckx, O.P., "Ingreja ou Igrejas?," in V. A., *Cinco problemas que desafiam a Igreja hoje*, pp. 26ff.
[9] Taken from *Vatican II: The Work That Needs to Be Done*, edited by David Tracy with Hans Küng and Johann Metz (New York: Concilium, Seabury Press, 1978), p. 91, emphasis added.

Küng. During that speech, the Cardinal mentioned the Catechism of St. Pius X. This superb catechism defines the Church of Christ according to the traditional definition given by St. Robert Bellarmine; that the Catholic Church is a "perfect society." It is the community of men professing the same true Christian Faith, sharing the same sacraments, under the governance of one head, the Vicar of Christ on earth. Cardinal Sodano said that this definition of the Church is rather "narrow" according to today's standards.[10] Fr. Joseph Ratzinger voiced similar statements in 1966. He praised Vatican II's broader definition of the Church and disparaged Bellarmine's definition as a "very narrow formulation."[11]

Thirty-four years later, Cardinal Ratzinger spoke without reservation of Vatican II's new definition of the Church. He said, "Vatican II did not use Pius XII's expression according to which 'the Roman Catholic Church is the only Church of Christ.' Instead, it preferred the expression 'The Church of Christ subsists in the Catholic Church...' because," he said, "it wished to affirm that the being of the Church as such is a larger identity than the Roman Catholic Church."[12]

The New Mass is a reflection of the new ecclesiology, and the progressivists in power are well aware of this fact. It explains their aversion to the old Latin Liturgy.

In October 1976, Dr. Eric de Saventhem, then president of Una Voce, held an interview with Archbishop (later Cardinal) Benelli in Rome. When Dr. de Saventhem pointed to widespread liturgical chaos and asked how the suppression of the old Mass could be justified, Benelli told him that "those who wish to retain the old Mass have a different ecclesiology"–in other words, the traditional and true definition of the Church.

Likewise in 1998 Michel Semin, then director of the Czech Una Voce Chapter, approached Prague's Cardinal Vlk asking

---

[10] The story is found in J. Vennari, "Vatican Praises Purveyor of Heresy," *Fatima Crusader*, Spring-Summer, 1998.

[11] Joseph Ratzinger, *Theological Highlights of Vatican II* (New York: Paulist Press, 1966), pp. 65-66.

[12] *Frankfurter Allgemeine*, English translation taken from newsletter of Fr. Jean Violette, SSPX, District Superior of Canada, Toronto, October, 2000.

for a weekly Tridentine Mass. Vlk flatly refused, saying that he would never allow the Tridentine Mass because he sees his job as Cardinal-Archbishop to implement the *new ecclesiology* of Vatican II.

The fact that we have been given a "new definition" of the Church means that we have been given a new religion. Now, there are three main elements to religion: doctrine, morals, and worship.

1) Doctrine: those truths which we believe;
2) Morals: how we behave based on those beliefs;
3) Worship: how we pay homage to our God based on what we know of Him.

We see that *doctrine* is the most important, since morals are the fruit of doctrine and liturgy (worship) is the expression of doctrine. Thus, Mohammedans do not pray to Jesus Christ in their religious rituals because they do not believe that Jesus Christ is God. We will never see a Jew bless himself in the name of the Father and of the Son and of the Holy Ghost because the Jew does not believe in God as Trinity. Likewise, the architects of the New Mass did not give us a liturgy that is exclusively Catholic because they do not believe that the Church of Christ is exclusively Catholic. This is one of the main reasons why I have drawn a line in the sand between the old Mass and the new Mass, and I never attend the new rite. Vatican II gave us a new ecumenical religion, and the new liturgy is the *fruit* of that new religion.

The First Commandment says, "I am the Lord thy God; thou shalt not have strange gods before Me." This being the case, it is clear that no authority in the Church can make us accept a new liturgy that has steered away from the true religion in order to pay homage to the strange god of ecumenism.

Buried Treasure

Yet there is more to all this than disparaging the New Mass with its silliness and shenanigans. Adherence to the true Mass brings with it a superabundance of graces and benefits beyond our calculation. As for the supernatural benefits, I cannot do better than quote St. John Vianney: "If we understood what the Mass really is, we would die of love."

Aside from this truth, one of the prime personal advantages of adhering to the Old Mass was that it inspired me to search for buried treasure. Once we find the true Mass that revolutionary men have taken from us, we begin to hunt for other aspects of the Faith that were taken from us as well. We want the *entire Catholic patrimony*, not simply the Old Mass alone.

The rediscovering of the true Mass led me to a search for genuine Catholic doctrine, a fuller knowledge and understanding of the Catholic Faith of all time as taught consistently throughout the centuries prior to Vatican II. It led to a search for true Catholic moral theology. In a sense I had been looking for this even before I found the Old Mass, due to the absence of–and perversion of–Catholic morals presented to me in high school.

Discovery of the true Mass also led me to seek the true Catholic philosophy of St. Thomas Aquinas. In the pursuit, I met great philosophers along the way, including the renowned Fr. Garrigou-Lagrange, who predicted in the mid-1940's that the "new theology" of Henri de Lubac, Maurice Blondel and others of their species would lead the Church straight back to Modernism. This new theology triumphed at Vatican II,[13] and neo-Modernism has corrupted and disfigured the Church ever since, just as Fr. Garrigou-Lagrange predicted. This gave me an appreciation of true Thomistic philosophy as a magnificent means for the recognition of truth and diagnostic of error. It is a system that gives human reason the tools to recognize bad principles and to accurately predict the consequences of these principles. Thomism liberates us from the dreamy sentimentalism that is the hallmark of our age.

The pursuit of buried treasure also led me to Pope Pius IX's magnificent Syllabus of Errors, St. Pius X's masterful censure of Modernism, and to the manly condemnation of religious indiffer-

---

[13] Fr. Henrici, a disciple of the New Theology, boasted that the "New Theology" triumphed at Vatican II. See "They Think They Have Won," *SISINONO*, August, 1993–October, 1994.

entism and "liberal Catholicism" by the great Popes of the nineteenth and early twentieth century.

Another treasure I discovered was the true papal doctrine on the social Kingship of Jesus Christ, which teaches that states, governments and social institutions have the objective duty to recognize the Catholic religion as the one true Church of Our Lord and to treat it accordingly. Along with this is the objective duty of governments to base their laws of right and wrong on what the Gospel and the Church teach is right and wrong. No part of God's creation is exempt from God's law. States, governments and social institutions are part of God's creation. Thus states, governments and social institutions are not exempt from God's law. It is a remarkably simple truth, yet it was never taught to me during my entire twelve years in Catholic school.

All of this led me to recognize the post-conciliar crisis of faith as one of the easiest crises to live through in history. The modernist conciliar theologians are not really original thinkers. For the most part, all they have done is rehash old errors already condemned, which are easily countered by the writings of the pre-Vatican II popes, particularly the anti-liberal popes from 1800 to 1958. The errors of Vatican II's ecumenism and religious liberty—which are inherent in the Council documents—are *already answered* by the popes' condemnations of religious indifferentism, of false notions regarding human liberty, and of separation of Church and State. The error of Vatican II's "updating" of the Catholic religion is *already answered* by Pope St. Pius X's condemnation of Modernism, and by Vatican Council I, which states infallibly that Catholics are bound to adhere to the Catholic Faith as it has always been taught, "in the same sense and in the same meaning."[14]

Thus, my return to the Latin Mass and subsequent hunt for buried treasure brought me to the entirety of the Catholic Faith in all its beauty. I use the term beauty not in a sentimental manner, but in the Thomistic sense of the word. The intellect is sat-

---

[14] See Vatican I's *Dei Filius* and Pius X's Oath Against Modernism.

isfied by that which is true. The will is satisfied by that which is good. This combination of the true and the good constitutes the beautiful: "That which is seen, pleases."[15] There can be nothing on earth more true, more good, and thus more beautiful, than the Catholic Faith given by God in its fullness and the Holy Sacrifice of the Mass as a true expression of the Faith, a reflection of heaven, and a re-presentation of Christ's supreme Sacrifice on the Cross for our redemption.

> John Vennari spent fourteen years at Holy Family Monastery, where he wrote the regular *Crying in the Wilderness* newsletter. He is editor of the traditional monthly newspaper, *Catholic Family News*.

---

[15] *Summa Theologica*, I, Q. 5, Art. 4, ad 1.

Dr. Andrew Childs

Breaking the Silence: A Conversion to Truth through Music

> You have made us for yourself, and our heart is restless until it rests in you.
> —St. Augustine, *Confessions*[1]

All versions of the realization of God have the same essence: the variations depend on prefix and circumstance. The *con*-version story involves a change in character, perspective, and state: having accepted and followed one manner of living and believing, the convert accepts another and changes course. Though he remains the same vessel, he empties himself of any previous cargo and forsakes his previous destination, at times indistinguishable from—and yet still dependent upon—his former self. No less dramatic, stories of "*re*-version" depicting a return of the prodigal to God simultaneously inspire hope and highlight the potential frailty of human faithfulness. Some who share these pages will relate "return to tradition" stories, having endured the singular disorientation of the anti-prodigal, who remained home alone when all of existence—father, mother, brother, farm, fatted calf and all—seemed to vanish into the humanist fog.

A version is a particular account, and every particular account of turning to face eternal Truth shares two elements: a unique initial orientation and a common focal point. We find consolation and confirmation in the infinitely variable individual descriptions

---

[1] *The Confessions of Saint Augustine*, Msgr. John K. Ryan, trans. and ed. (New York: Doubleday, 1960), 1.1, p. 43. All chapter headings and translations come from this edition.

of perspective, catalysts, pacing, duration, and unpredictability of such turnings, as well as in the universality of personal experience and common destiny in God. We want to know how others came to know what we know, and the particulars fascinate. In the end, we sustain each other, collectively representing the totality of questions and answers we may face—as well as the highs and lows we will endure—throughout the fight. Without this support, the prospect of continuing to fight could easily overwhelm—something vital to remember given the fact that every living version remains unfinished. What part I have to relate follows, and in crooked lines; an echo of an ever present past.

> *The psychology of infancy:* "*I have never seen anyone knowingly throw aside the good when he purges the bad.*"—Confessions, 1:7

I was not born Catholic, yet I chose as the product of a non-Catholic formation to embrace the Catholic Faith. In recognizing a change in mindset from my pre-Catholic days, I try to avoid the temptation to assume that no good existed in my 'former' state due to its lack of Catholicity. Simply put, God willed my past as necessary for my present—and as a reminder of the uncertainty of my future. My mother was born Catholic, and a Catholic heritage does provide a sort of momentum: as part of an extended Catholic family, my process of discovery merged with a story already in progress. Though the Church's abandonment of itself took its toll on my mother as it did on everyone of her generation (my parents married in the early 1960's), she nonetheless transmitted a subtle but consistent familiarity with Catholicism to my four siblings and me. Mixed marriages succeed against supernatural odds, and the harvest of the Church's "new springtime" includes the failure of my parents' marriage; in a climate other than that of Vatican II, however, they likely never would have married and I would not exist.

Those born Catholic learn from the first question of their catechism that the Church directs us before anything else *to know*. The Catholic Faith exists ultimately as an exercise of intellect and of will. I can look back on my upbringing in rural northern New Hampshire and recognize with real fondness and appreciation how much it prepared me to know and accept Truth when challenged with it. God would not appeal to me *to know* through the formal religion of my childhood, but I would never deny the impact made on me by the morality, ethics, and familiarity with Scripture that underpin New England Protestantism. The Church did not direct those who educated me in public schools, yet they did so with competence, sincere good will, and an adherence to traditional methods found only in small towns too remote and sensible to feel compelled by educational trends. My education prepared me to know, but lacking proper motivation and a sense of proper ends, I should have learned much more than I did.

God's first appeal to me came through natural beauty. Though I know—and have always known—that the Transcendentalists' approach to communing with God through nature falls short of religion, having grown up surrounded by physical beauty, I understand Emerson as he writes in "Nature" that "In the woods we return to reason and faith. There I feel that nothing can befall me in life—no disgrace, no calamity (leaving me my eyes), which nature cannot repair." The flaw in New England Transcendentalism lies not in its suggestion of nature as a tangible expression of an intangible universal, but in its extension of natural beauty to the state of human existence—assuming a sort of blameless inborn majesty and reflection of divinity in the human creature—and, given man's undeniable need to worship in the proper sense, in its failing to recognize the moral peril in nature-worship: nature takes on many forms, many quite dangerous. For the "lover of nature," sensuality and religiosity often become indistinguishable.

> *"It is not the infant's will that is harmless, but the weakness of infant limbs."* –Confessions, 1:7

As a lover of nature, I sought to optimize my appreciation of it through various physical and intellectual experiences, having been blessed with certain talents and precocious tastes. I enjoyed sophistication, and found not only that standard adolescent pursuits held comparatively little interest for me, but also that given the fact that they engaged most of my peers, I had little competition in my quest for adult experiences and found many adults who, fascinated by my occupying the realm of their recreation, happily facilitated my development. I began, as children do in all seriousness, to put on adult clothing.

I progressed in good things and bad. For the good, I developed at an accelerated rate an appreciation of created beauty in all realms due to my associations and inclinations. As for the bad, I am grateful that youthful sophistication has its limits: though I had no desire to avoid the perils which resulted from excesses and abuse of good things, I had firstly a limited practical capacity to indulge; secondly, the good fortune of a sort of temperance by extension (I realize gratefully in retrospect that the adults who guided me would frequently, and often very artfully, prevent me from making truly disastrous choices); and lastly and most ironically–can we doubt God's goodness and paternal patience with us?–the sort of disproportionate pride found only in self-appointed "exceptional" adolescents that left me too convinced of my own superiority and vastness of understanding to realize how much more peril I could have faced had I truly known what I *knew* I knew.

Here an important point. An increase in sophistication or culture in many cases involves appreciation of–or perfection in–morally indifferent activities, neither edifying nor perilous in their nature: food, drink, music, art, sports, *etc.* Context and intention frequently define morality, and I would use my "cautionary" tale not as grounds to avoid either sophistication or cultivation, but rather to encourage them. When I failed to avoid certain dangers in certain instances, this related to my lack of Catholic perspective rather than any inherent badness of my activities. Because I could not recognize my pride as such, I remained wrongly convinced that my advanced tastes proved the maturity both of my appetites and my control over them. The current obsession with maintaining attachments to childish or adolescent tastes and approaches proves almost universally disastrous because it encourages downward developmental movement toward ignorance and vulgarity. In my far more dangerous case, however, though I sought 'transcendent' experiences, I ignored the adolescent nature of my over-indulgence because I consumed such refined delicacies.

Catholics must not excuse ignorance in the form of a willful lack of sophistication, ultimately a form either of intellectual sloth or the pride of false humility. This isolation cuts us off from our Catholic heritage as proper arbiters of truth and beauty. However, though ultimately unjustifiable, a lack of sophistication seems a reasonable approach when faced with the false but panic-inducing prospect of having to abandon Catholic heritage *for the sake* of sophistication. Truth and beauty belong to God; knowledge of Faith provides balance and contextual focus. God wills that we have for our proper enjoyment all licit manner of beauty. My temperament, talents, and the circumstances of my upbringing allowed me extraordinary contact with all types of transcendent natural and created beauty, but by failing to see God in them, I turned these gifts into weapons through my fault alone.

> *Good out of evil: "You have ordered it, and so it is,
> that every disordered mind should be
> its own punishment."*–Confessions, 1:12

The punishment is twofold: first, in that disorder begets disorder, and as one of the marks of chaos in such a mind, disorder seems to become a sort of order in its predictability–a dependable and ultimately depended upon sort of misery. The second punishment relates to the continual awareness in the mind ordered by Faith of its previous disorder; in the extreme, the present becomes lost to the past in despair of the future. Yet justice necessitates the punishment, and mercy pervades it; we superimpose severity on our recollection. God in His mercy allows us to keep the memory of our faults close at hand, not as a continual source of danger, but as a licit and powerful way to contemplate certain of our faults for purposes of advancement and avoidance.

A Student…

I decided to go to college in southern California as a calculated act of indifference in reaction to what I perceived as total failure. I knew of the University of California system, but California seemed a distant, not quite real, and not particularly serious place for a self-assured New Englander of Ivy League lineage. Plenty of people lived in the "land of fruit and nuts" but mostly, as I had always heard, old hippies, young hippies, surfers, and movie stars; America contracted the business of life on the east coast, and given that, in my adolescent opinion, only a chosen few professions could properly reflect the superabundance of my potential, I decided on the course of my future life: Ivy League, but not Harvard (my father and older sister went there—I was special, and so chose to allow Dartmouth College to serve my purposes), and not in medicine (again, father, uncle, cousin, eventually older and younger sisters—my specialness needed space within the family circle to reflect its splendor...); some sort of undergraduate degree frolicked in with the intention of moving on directly and doubtless with great fanfare to Harvard Business School, then onward to an undefined but splendiferous (but short) business career involving Machiavellian power and wealth of Brobdingnagian proportions. I would marry an heiress with a heart of gold who recognized my intellectual greatness, we would have twin daughters—on whose sixteenth birthdays I would buy matching Jaguar convertibles—and a Rottweiler named Nigel that would ride next to me in my private golf cart as I played brilliantly in breathtaking locales. My siblings and our families would gather in one of my mansions and we would discuss great things over expensive wine after I had cooked a magnificent gourmet meal. On Sundays in the fall, we would all don L.L. Bean and Talbots and walk through the fallen leaves and the crispness of the New England Indian summer, and in the evening perhaps attend some cultural event—further enhancing our stature as Renaissance paragons—that I would expertly critique, having lately come to the realization that I possessed dazzling artistic gifts on top of all the rest.

 God of mercy and vision of all things and ages in an eternal present; God whose mere thought of us becomes our life in time and eternal destiny—what greater mercy do You manifest than to save us from our own determination? Nearly everything that I love most now–Faith and family–exists specifically as the result of my failing to achieve anything I had wanted so badly at the time of life when young people casually choose what past they will look back on. Growing up with great success in a small and best part of my small world, I had assumed certain things about my ability to make myself. God Who made me would unmake my self-making, and allow my pride to facilitate my undoing. Though certainly qualified to follow the path I had chosen in life, when I turned to start my journey, I found the doors I had assumed would open to me firmly shut. As the fourth of five eventual high school valedictorians, brother of physicians and leaders of men, a son of legacy– I had the singular distinction as the only member of my nuclear tribe not to get into college. Granted, I had only really applied to one place, but with every reason to expect success; Dartmouth simply failed to recognize its responsibility to my greatness.

Love for the Lost Friend: "I marveled that other men should live, because he, whom I had loved as if he would never die, was dead. I marveled more that I, his second self, could live when he was dead."–Confessions, 4:6

I mourned what I saw as the death of my future self with the disproportionate gravity of a child. Augustine mourned the death of his friend: what more intimate friend do we have than our conception of our future self? On whom do we depend more? Convinced of its demise, whose death could we mourn more severely than that of this conceived reality of ourselves, given the fact that we remain alive to grieve? Our Faith speaks of the joy of dying to ourselves, but when our future dies and we lack the consolations of Faith and trust in Divine Providence, joy seems impossible. Despair and self-pity loom large, yet God's patience and mercy loom larger. Time healed, God remained silent, and unfortunately, I found reasonable comfort in my customary distractions.

Soon enough, the sting of the death of my former future self lessened, and I felt the awkward relief of one who no longer has to care for a terminally ill friend. I still loved my friend, and never lost a sense of reverence and regret for what I would not become, but convinced of the impossibility of that possibility, I soon habituated to a newfound freedom, one known only to those who manage to engineer for themselves a life of responsible irresponsibility. Having prepared myself for the burden of industry captaincy, the comparatively weightless mantel of bartender, cook, tennis pro, and auto parts delivery truck driver (had I mentioned the diversity of my talents?) allowed my spirit to soar...and provided just enough cash to finance my amusements. Yet I knew somehow that I could not live this way forever. The bony finger of responsibility beckoned, but the mourning I had undergone for my recently passed former future self had turned to resentment; my pride would not allow me to follow the path I had formerly chosen. I knew that whatever future emerged would require college education, and motivated in large part by the twin Narcissistic virtues of indignation and spite–and strangely invigorated by my late Bohemianism–I set off to form my future past in the land of fruit and nuts.

"Thus saith the Lord..."

Having accumulated enough credits as a high school junior to graduate, my senior year proved difficult in terms of scheduling classes. My younger sister in effect dared me to sing in the choir–something not seen as a masculine pursuit–and, given the fact that few other class offerings existed, I took her up on it. I was grateful for having done this when it came time to register for college classes because, unable for reasons of priority enrollment and lack of specified major to register for the required full load of classes, it occurred to me to register for a two-credit choir. My audition for this choir consisted of an awkward conversation with the head of the department: What would I sing for my audition, he asked? (Audition, I thought?) Nothing prepared, I said. Surely you know something, he said. Well, something, I said, but surely you don't want to hear it–it's just something I sing along with in the car, I said. Try me, he said, and so I began to imitate, as I frequently did in the car–with, as it turned out, a sort of accuracy shocking to my new friend–the precise timbre, phrasing, nuance, and vocal idiosyncrasies of the middle-aged British baritone John

Shirley-Quirk singing the florid recitative "Thus saith the Lord" from Handel's *Messiah*. No big deal, thought I (the aforementioned senior year included some free periods during which I would sit in the choir director's office and sing along to some of his recordings: I had gotten pretty good at Shirley-Quirk). *Big* deal, thought my new department head: before I left his office he had made arrangements with the registrar for me to become a major in music. I had no idea one could major in a hobby, but given my new outlook on life—and I was in California, for goodness' sake—a music major I became. I rejoiced in my newfound responsible irresponsibility as a hobby major not knowing that God had allowed me to break His silence: having through sensual experience long understood in natural terms the truth of God's beauty, I would now come to appreciate—through sounds that overwhelmed, intellectually and emotionally—the beauty of God's Truth. Though I did not yet turn to the Church, I began to understand the metaphysical essence of transcendence through sounds and their effects on me. I had converted to Truth through music.

"*Immer leiser wird mein Schlummer...*"
At certain points each year, my internal thermostat—permanently calibrated to northern New England—senses the utter wrongness of other climates: most are too hot too soon for too long, and with altogether too much sunshine. Having come to the University of California, Irvine (some fifty miles or so south of Los Angeles) I found the weather charming, but thoroughly superficial: cloudless skies and eighty degrees seemed quaint for a few weeks, but surely some weather of substance had to exist— the character-building sanity of a forty-degree temperature drop over the course of an afternoon, a perspective-affirming sub-zero Arctic air mass settling in for a few weeks, or perhaps the consoling thoughtfulness of a month or two of overcast skies. No such luck. Instead, I faced day after day of the same meteorological assault—sun, heat, sun, heat—and like a man staggering delirious through the desert, I sought refuge where I could, often in the sane confines of dark, air-conditioned lecture halls. I would go

Love in the Ruins

from one such place to the next, unwittingly auditing some fascinating classes, and growling at fellow students babbling about going to the beach or some other vapid nonsense. Wandering through the Fine Arts complex on a typically awful beautiful southern California day, I found more than I had bargained for.

Life-changing experiences happen. When they do, participants undergo reconfiguration seemingly on the particulate level; the event engulfs on every cognitive and sensational plane, including the perception of the passage of time. Mystical theology provides examples of ecstasies in which participants experience dimensions of consciousness unaccountable by linear time and normal sensational capacity–true glimpses of the infinite...mostly, those who experience life-changing events have the good sense to keep them to themselves. The actual events, in many cases, are quite small things, catalysts igniting a sort of metaphysical flare. In a moment of pure brilliance, these illuminate some otherwise impenetrably darkened recess, the revelation of which necessitates instantaneous and permanent change.

On the stage of a darkened concert hall a woman I didn't know sang a song in a language I didn't understand by a composer I had never heard of, and she and a pianist created an atmosphere of sound so astonishingly beautiful that I could neither breathe nor consider the possibility in my head or heart of any other thing; I had become entirely lost to myself in a soundscape that I had no capacity to measure or contain, the effects of which made me wonder if I had ever felt anything at all, the simultaneous newness and overwhelming familiarity of which caused me to wonder if I knew anything other than my need to feel and hear what I did at that moment. I had the realization of my total fluency in an emotional language I had never spoken, and recognized only then that I had been journeying my entire life to find this home where I had never been. Johannes Brahms died in 1897. He wrote the song "Immer leiser wird mein Schlummer" in 1886; it lasts roughly four minutes. I heard it for the first time on that day in 1988, and knew somehow I needed to do to others what this woman had done to me, because this meant something truly

Dr. Andrew Childs

and intimately important: the ability to give to others profound and necessary knowledge of themselves and their world through the expression of Truth made manifest in musical beauty. Though I had not yet come home to the Faith, I had converted to metaphysics–and metaphysical altruism–through musical performance.

> *False Philosophy and False Theology:* "*I despaired, O Lord of heaven and earth, creator of all things visible and invisible, of finding the truth within your Church, from which they had averted me.*"–Confessions, 5:10

Music brought me to formal religion, but not at first to the Church. I had overcome some of the standard youthful arrogance obligatory for undergraduates educated in a climate of secular humanism, which assumed that, in the words of Isaiah Berlin–a darling of the liberal intelligentsia–Enlightenment rationalism had successfully rendered religion obsolete as a "chaotic amalgam of ignorance, mental laziness, guesswork, superstition, prejudice, dogma, fantasy, and above all, the 'interested error' maintained by the rulers of mankind and largely responsible for the blunders, vices, and misfortunes of humanity." Charming and invigorating nonsense when trying to impress young feminists at cocktail parties, but not a serious answer to the serious questions raised by the obvious existence of absolutes, and intellectual and moral conflict.

As a professional musician and graduate student having grown up outside the Catholic form, many things averted me, primary among them modern Catholic liturgical music–as the direct, grotesque, and debased opposite of the millennium-old tradition of sublime and definitive church music I had studied as art–which stands as one of the most egregious examples of a reversal of substantive formal principles in the history of artistic expression. This is incontrovertible fact. To abandon Gregorian chant, sacred monophony, polyphonic organum, the Masses of Palestrina and Byrd, the polyphonic motets of Josquin, Victoria, and Schütz, the majesty of Gabrieli's *canzoni* with multiple choirs and brass, the kaleidoscopic harmonic textures of Gesualdo's *Tenebrae*, the Masses of Beethoven, Haydn, Mozart, Schubert, Bruckner, and the requiems of Ockeghem, Lassus, Palestrina, Victoria, Verdi,

Love in the Ruins

Berlioz, Fauré, Duruflé, Mozart–for what? "*Michael row the boat ashore*" or two buffoons–doubtless well-intentioned–with a guitar and a drum set spraying sentimental adolescent pop-music sewage into the sanctuary? As a performer understanding the importance of inspirational majesty as well as aesthetic and dramatic cohesion in liturgy, the music of the modern Catholic Church did not indicate an institution more in touch with itself and the world; it indicated an institution that had lost its mind. Most modern Catholic service music is insultingly bad–*comically* bad–in itself; beyond this, any claim it makes of inheritance to the tradition of epic Catholic musical art represents–in purely natural terms–a greater liturgical scandal than the New Mass, which adheres more closely to the *Missale Romanum* that does the *Weekly Missalette* to the *Liber Usualis*. If only for reasons of aesthetic sanity, I would look elsewhere for my Christianity.

Anglicanism, as a priest friend of mine has remarked, suggests in effect the possibility of "salvation through good taste." A statement as poignant as it is flippant, the High Anglican Church in America exists as a religion of thoughtful people with exceptional appreciation for liturgical aesthetics and natural virtue caught in the crossfire of opposing liberal social agendas in a shoot-out with the uncomfortably inflexible morality of traditional Christianity. In Seattle, I joined a community of 'Anglican Catholics' as they called themselves, who assisted my discovery of the depth of Catholic thought, the vitality of Augustine, Bede, and Aquinas. Many had difficulty assigning to their Catholicity the qualifier "Anglican": simply Catholic, they insisted, without the reliance on the specific traditional office of the papacy, and besides, they would argue in support of their approach to traditional religious heritage, who better defends orthodoxy in liturgy? Who better indeed: the Catholic musical tradition covets nothing of its Anglican counterpart, but an admiring acknowledgment could pass between the two. The Anglicans have a magnificent musical tradition I remain grateful to know. As saddened as I became at the realizations that my personal attachments to my Anglican friends could not cover the multitude of doctrinal inconsistencies I discovered, I knew, as a convert to Truth through beauty, that God in His mercy had allowed an accumulation of beauty in Anglican music sufficient to catalyze the tendencies of anyone similarly inclined to conversion by it. I had converted to Liturgy and Christian thought through Anglicanism. Aesthetically and socially, I could have remained quite comfortable in it. God had previously allowed me to break His silence with music. He would now no longer allow the progress of comfort and error developing around my tightening embrace of his Faith. I would meet two men—one of whom I thought I knew as I knew myself, though not, I would discover, the man of Faith he had become—who have to my knowledge never remained silent about the One True Faith since their respective conversions.

The relative and the absolute:
"I asked, 'What is iniquity?' and I found that it is not a substance.
It is a perversity of will...."–Confessions, 7:16

Someone begat David Allen White the convert, who in turn begat many of the converts many of us know, including my brother Matthew the convert who in turn turned to the business of begetting my converted self. So these things go. As social creatures, God has allowed us to serve the purpose of some usefulness to each other—leaving us, however, to our own stylist devices. In the case of both men—my fellow performer the good Doctor with his lion mouth and spirit, and, in the depth of our melancholy, my metaphysical-twin brother—if either had any previous acquaintance with subtlety in personal discourse, both summarily ignored it during their splendid tag-team pummeling of my nascent denominationalism. Over the course of a social evening in Annapolis, a conversation to this effect took place. The lion bellowed, "Religion, eh?" "Yes, Anglicanism seems to me the most reasonable option what with, well, bad things happening to good people and all—and the music, you know...," I offered, politely sipping a martini. "Circumstance can't transgress justice; and besides your argument ignores the causational issue of free will," my brother stated flatly, having purposefully made my martini far too dry and with a twist of lemon–I could feel myself becoming parched. "What," continued my brother, "of the obvious discrepancy with…" "Yes, yes, music, but how do you propose," interrupted the lion, taking a stout leonine gulp of his drink before casually detonating the one unanswerable objection to the concept of Anglicanism, Catholic or otherwise, "to found a religion on the lust of a King? Jolly good brie!" he roared as the conversation continued with a matter-of-factness that felt like the intellectual equivalent of a pat on the head. And so it went on until the gin ran out.

The personal love of friendship will not always survive challenges of ideas; friends in serious enough opposition–that which surpasses the possibility of 'agreeing to disagree'–simply cease to remain friends. Relatives in similar opposition face much greater stakes. I realize the risk my brother took in this and subsequent conversations in challenging the superficiality of my belief, knowing both the ultimately emotional nature of the impediments that underlay my reluctance to embrace traditional Catholicism, and the severity with which I would likely react to his ideological dismantling of these impediments and the predictable compromises surrounding my belief because of them. He persisted. My initial reaction, less defensive than it could have been, led to the final step in my acceptance of One, Holy, Catholic, and Apostolic religion.

The Voice as of a child:
"Take up and read…."–Confessions, 8:12

With humble confidence and faith, Augustine opened a book of Scripture to find God's specific admonition to him. Still enough myself to find inspiration in spite and indignation, I took up books to read–not with the intention of increasing the depth of my knowledge of the Faith, but of justifying myself through research. I fell into the trap my brother had set for me (likely one previously set for him) not in an attempt to avoid debate or insult me, but rather, recognizing in me some intellectual objectivity, to have me settle the matter for myself on the level of truth. The undeniable challenge: prove it wrong.

Here I have to pause. I find it hard to relive even in synopsis the efforts I expended, the agonies of realization—what I had become, the devastation I had wrought, the pain caused, the state I could have died in, the length and distance of the journey I had taken at full speed away from the God I now pretended to love on my own terms—the foolishness, the pride, and the death throes of my final former selves. I felt confident I would gain my freedom in a matter of hours or perhaps days—one contradiction on the level of faith, morals, or doctrine would suffice, my brother assured. I set out to disprove Truth, the *"Truth that will make you free."* [2]

The quest that began in spite and pride from outside the Faith continues in humility and urgency from within it. None can find any such contradiction in faith, morals, or doctrine, but questions persist, and attacks continue; family and friends, and a world of those desperate for the freedom of God's Truth still subsist outside of it. I no longer seek to disprove that for which no dis-proof exists; I seek to compensate for all the time I wasted in ignorance of the first precept of my Faith. If God has determined for me *to know*, I must transmit how I know what I know and to what end. The God of nature, and beauty, and Truth, and religion will come to those who know Him through all these things if with the simplicity of a child—and the humility of an adult struggling to abandon childish adherence to willfulness and pride—they will submit to Him in them.

> *Music as means and end: "Thus do I waver*
> *between the danger of sensual pleasure*
> *and wholesome experience."*—Confessions, 10:33

I am a man lately born a Catholic. As such, my vocation has changed from one of turning wholesomeness toward sensuality, to one of ennobling sensuality through the wholesome and intelligent conscription of sensual experience through Catholic understanding. I cannot deny the power of my previous experience and formation, which enabled me to glimpse the infinite through the finite means of artistic creation and the human capacity to

---

[2] Jn. 8:32.

comprehend it: what remained for me then, and what I strive so passionately to communicate now, was the interpretation of these human expressions of Divine inspiration through Catholic means and for Catholic ends. We can neither deny our sensual capacity, nor abandon our senses to it. *All truth and beauty belong to God*: He would have us know, love and serve Him through these vehicles of Truth expressed through beauty. When directed by faith and reason, few more effective pathways to transcendence exist.

The Only Gateway: "*At your door let us knock for it…*"–Confessions, 13:38

I took on the light burden of Faith on the first of March, 1997, at the Seminary of St. Thomas Aquinas, Winona, Minnesota, received into the Church by a bishop of the Roman Catholic Church ordained by Archbishop Marcel Lefebvre, who by such consecration handed down what he had received, the utter adherence and faithfulness to the fullness of the teaching and sanctifying capacity of Eternal Rome. In this way, I became a member of the body of faithful souls bound to persist in the temporal quest to possess and maintain sanctifying grace for the purpose of attaining eternity with God.

I sought beauty, and God allowed me to find Truth; through Truth God allowed me to find the Church. I came to the Church, and the Church asked me what I would have of her–I asked that she give me Faith, the key to reconciliation of former toils, to purpose in the present struggle, to trust and surrender to God's Providence. What we *know* is Faith, and every version, every particular account leads to this; arrival at the only gateway. But what an arrival…lest I am tempted to feel any sense of personal accomplishment in having arrived here, I look back on my crooked past. I realize to my great surprise that it led nowhere–God put the gate in front of me.

Dr. Andrew Childs serves currently as Associate Dean and Chair of Humanities at St. Mary's College, and Assistant to the Director of Education for the United States District of the Society of Saint Pius X (SSPX). Previously, he taught at Yale University, Missouri State

Dr. Andrew Childs

University, the Thames Valley Music School at Connecticut College, and was Managing Coordinator of the Department of Voice and Opera at the Yale School of Music. He has sung over one hundred performances of nearly thirty operatic roles, as well as much of the major concert repertoire with orchestras throughout the country. He made his Lincoln Center debut in 1999, and has to his credit a world premiere by a Pulitzer Prize-winning composer. Centaur Records released his solo disc of Charles Ives songs in 2006, about which the American Record Guide stated, "…there is no better recording by a tenor." Dr. Childs lives in St. Mary's, Kansas, with his wife Krista, their children, and two cats of legendary girth and good nature.

Dr. David Allen White

"Shadow" Sacraments

As our sun sets, we reflect more and more on our earliest sunrise. We should not be surprised that as we age, our thoughts return with greater frequency to our earliest days; our grandparents retreated there, our aging neighbors regale us with memories of departed times and even in our middle years our thoughts have led us back to our high school days (hence the greater numbers of surviving classmates who attend each subsequent reunion). My thoughts of late have been dwelling on the church in which I was raised, an impressive stone structure of imposing dignity in Eau Claire, Wisconsin. Sadly, the weighty exterior was hiding emptiness within, for this was a liberal Protestant church; this was a church without sacraments.

Much good came from my years there. I met and knew many good souls; I learned by heart numerous passages from Scripture; I received the fundamentals of musical education which the public schools, even then, viewed as ornamental and unnecessary. But I had no sacramental life, nor did I have any knowledge of what a sacrament actually was. The Sunday morning worship consisted of Bible readings, hymn singing, a long sermon and more music from the choir. Occasionally there was a strange part of the service called "communion" during which the ushers would distribute tiny elf glasses of grape juice and shiny plates of cubed airy-dough white bread (the only "Wonder" of the ceremony). I did not know why, and my only interest in this peculiar proceeding centered on my own anticipation of a sound. After the congregation had imbibed the Welch's juice cup, they all in a simultaneous gesture placed them in the small wooden cup holders affixed to the back of each pew. The hundreds of crystalline echoes of thin glass clinging and clicking against the wooden holes made a magical sound and in that I took delight. But it was magical sound without meaning.

I am told I was baptized in that church but, of course, I have no memory of it. Baptism is one of the two sacraments carried over by the Protestants when they revolted against Holy Mother Church and wandered off on their own to then divide into thousands of individual and contradictory sects. The other is marriage. These two remained acceptable because they required no priest. Baptism can be performed by anyone as long as the water is poured across the forehead and the correct words are uttered, "I baptize thee in the name of the Father and the Son and the Holy Ghost." (As I was hardly self-aware at the time, I cannot be certain if I was baptized or not but if I was properly baptized correctly, I was baptized into the Catholic Church, the recipient and possessor of all of Christ's sacraments.)

Marriage is a vow taken between a man and a woman, and they themselves effect the sacrament. (As a life-long bachelor, I have never been blessed by that wonderful sacrament). The Protestants would allow these two sacraments to remain in their priest-free assemblies, but in doing so they confirm the validity of Christ's Church from which they broke away.

Curiously, though they refused to accept the other sacraments, they could not dismiss them completely, and so many of these sects have "shadow sacraments" that mimic the Catholic originals but, minus the priesthood and the proper forms and the proper matter and the proper intention, convey no grace. Such was the odd "communion" service I remember from my earliest days. The moment the emptiness of these "shadow" sacraments came home to me most clearly occurred when I received my "shadow" confirmation. In my teen years, I had received instruction in my "confirmation" class which prepared me for the signal day when I would be "confirmed." I have no memory whatsoever of anything I was taught in those classes that extended over many months, perhaps over many years. I can recall nothing; however, I do recall that no one could tell me what "confirmation" actually was. I had an inquiring mind, and inquiring minds want to know. That is why the young can often be pests. Anyone who has entered into that chain of inquiry with a child where every answer to a question is followed by the question "why?" will know how exasperating such quizzical youth can be. I kept asking "What is confirmation?" but the only answer I would get was that confirmation was the time when I would be confirmed. Seeing the frustration building in the adults around me, I stopped asking the question and lived with the uncertainty of not knowing why I was going through this training, much less what the end result would be. I not only had an inquiring mind, but I was imbued with a teleological desire, a need to know the final or end cause, which the wise old Greek Aristotle could have explained to my elders had he not been tainted by the praises of that Catholic theologian, St. Thomas Aquinas, who refers to his predecessor as "the Philosopher."

The big day arrived. My parents dutifully bought me a new suit and tie and on that most special Sunday of all Sundays, "Confirmation" Sunday, I was seated in a pew at the very front of the church with my fellow "confirmands." The usually long sermon proved to be even longer; the minister went on at length explaining the important step we were about to take in being "confirmed," but again he never really explained what that meant. We were to be "confirmed" in our faith and that faith was very important, but I was not very sure what that faith was, much less how I could be "confirmed" in it or what would be different about me or my faith once I was. And then the grand moment arrived. The pastor said, "Will the confirmands please rise." I dutifully stood with my fellows. He then solemnly announced, "You are now confirmed. Please be seated." We sat down. I was bewildered. What was that about? That was what I had gone to classes for over many months? What had happened? I was at sea.

I was at sea as a sitting duck. When, shortly thereafter, I went off to the University, I was a prime target for the shotgun pellets of doubt and scorn and hostility that were fired in nearly every class against what was simply called "religion." "Religion" was made to seem ridiculous, absurd, superstitious, empty, phony, the stuff of the stupid. To prove that I was "intelligent" I had to abandon such nonsense. I only needed to recall my "confirmation" service and I had to agree. I could see the church I had been raised in had really centered on social activities—church suppers, bake sales, picnics—and though many of the people I had known there had been models of decency, they had no serious religious foundation. And so what little faith I took with me into my years in higher education drifted away like down from a dead duck.

Death became my master. In class after class, I drank the poison cup poured for me by brilliant and assured professors. There was no moral order, man was free, all ethical evaluations were relative, sex was good, religion was bad, socialism was good, love of country was bad, family was constraining, the commune was liberating, the old was nonsense, the new was progress. These lessons I learned well for they were repeated to me from every side, and when I parroted them (despite what reservations my common sense might have raised against them), I prospered. When I hinted that I might not fully agree, I was scorned. There is an old Russian proverb that says, "When you run with the pack you may bark or not bark, but you must wag your tail." In the modern university, tail-wagging is insufficient; you had better bark, and your bark had better sound like the cacophonous cry of every other canine. You learn.

What you really learn is to follow the blind. And Our Lord stated precisely the result, "Can the blind lead the blind? Do they not both fall into the ditch?" In my thirtieth year, independent, successful and free, I awoke one morning to find myself in the gutter, if not the ditch. In the privacy of my room, I looked out over the beautiful expanse of Fairmount Park in Philadelphia, the city where in a local university I had been serving up the same poison, and stated simply, "I don't like myself anymore." In despair, I knelt by my bed and repeated the words of the Our Father, which I had been taught by my good parents many years before (may God bless them for that). What I still had to hold on to were those words, my family, my past, the beauties of nature, my love of music and poetry, my friends. Having implored God's help for the first time

Dr. David Allen White

in years, He responded with a lightning bolt, a brilliant student who began challenging everything I was saying in class. I intuited at once that my knowledge was nothing compared to what this young man had absorbed and so I would deliberately raise questions with him and take notes at the podium as he spoke. Occasionally, I would attempt to debate, but the debates would spill out of the classroom and continue in my office long after the sun had set.

This young man had been receiving instruction in the Catholic faith, but from a modernist priest whose instruction bore little connection to the doctrines and dogmas handed down by the Church over time. Every session became a battle for him with the young "instructee" insisting on Catholic dogma while the instructor priest denied it. Now that I was ready to take the same step (having realized the truth stated by the great Evelyn Waugh that the Catholic Church embodies a "coherent philosophical system that makes intransigent historical claims," in short, that all it taught was True), I was ready to "come inside" as well. Determined that I should not go through the agony of "instruction" he was enduring, my friend scoured the Philadelphia area for a devout Catholic priest who could give me solid instruction in the faith. He found good old Monsignor Michael Dean at St. Cyril of Alexandria's Church in East Landsdowne. Once a week I would board a train and head for St. Cyril's where I received serious instruction in the Catholic faith. On the evening of December 6, 1979, the Feast of St. Nicholas, Monsignor Dean conditionally rebaptized me, heard my first confession, and thus received me by means of these real sacraments into the Roman Catholic Church. As we walked around the great edifice (one filled with faith) in the dark of that brisk December night, this devout, kind man said to me, "You have come into the Church at the worst time in its history. When I was ordained a priest in 1940, I knew if another priest on the other side of the world made a statement on the faith, I could agree with it. Now, if a priest a few blocks away says something, I have to check it out first before I can give assent."

This holy man was one of many good religious who carried the burden of the New Church.

The next morning I took the train again out to the suburbs for morning Mass and my first Communion on the Feast of St. Ambrose (who would become my patron saint when I was finally really confirmed by Cardinal Krol in the Cathedral in Center City Philadelphia that spring). The Mass as celebrated by Monsignor Dean was solemn and dignified; he insisted that the faithful kneel for Communion, which he administered on the tongue. I later thought of this holy priest's Mass when I would encounter the words of Archbishop Marcel Lefebvre, who stated that the *Novus Ordo* Mass was not necessarily invalid.

Such Masses are rare as hen's teeth, however. For the next few years I attended local churches or churches where I happened to be visiting. What I experienced was a series of improbable, outlandish or idiotic occasions. Every modern Catholic can supply his own examples. I even found myself arguing with priests in the confessional as they minimized or excused what I knew to be serious sins, even storming out of a "chat session" (which often passes for confession in the New Church) after one such serious dispute, a dispute of eternal importance to my soul, I thought, and of minimal importance to "Fr. Bob." I felt as if I had returned to the church of "shadow" sacraments in which I had been raised; I felt like a drowning shipwrecked man who had reached the safety of a rescuing vessel only to discover that *that* ship was sinking. What finally drove me out of the New Church for good and all was not the guitar Mass or the twenty-two-minute Sunday Mass or the heresies in the homily, but rather two seemingly small outrages, but they were the two straws that broke this camel's back. First was the shock one Sunday of seeing one of the female midshipmen, one of my students, distributing Communion at Mass in the Naval Academy chapel. A sweet young thing, but hardly qualified to touch and dispense the body and blood of Our Lord Jesus Christ (*"Noli me tangere,"* Our Lord had said to St. Mary Magdalene, certainly more worthy to touch Him than Miss Middie), not to mention the inversion of authority to have a nine-

Dr. David Allen White

teen-year-old female giving the host to a professor at least twenty years her senior. This was Wonderland, not the Holy Roman Catholic Church. I made one last attempt, attending Mass at my local parish. There a cocktail pianist, playing sappy tunes that would be out of place in a decent piano bar, tipped me over the edge. Instead of putting my offering in the collection basket, I was tempted to drop it in a brandy snifter and set it on the piano. Enough. I left.

That summer I was visiting my parents in Wisconsin. My conscience continued to gnaw at me for I knew I had an obligation to "remember the Sabbath to keep it holy." My problem was that though I tried to remember the Sabbath, the new Mass and the endless shenanigans that surrounded it contained nothing holy. I always left having committed a serious sin—wrath. But I thought perhaps things would be calmer in the sleepy upper Midwest so I arose early one Sunday to drive to Mass at a parish I had known about for years but never attended. Praying my rosary and vaguely daydreaming, I arrived and found myself at the opposite end of town at another parish which I had no intention of visiting. I was puzzled and surprised, not aware that my guardian angel had been at the wheel. I saw a Mass was about to begin so I went in. An older, bantam-like, Irish priest came with great dignity to the altar accompanied by two serious young altar boys. He arranged things on the altar (ignoring the ubiquitous table) bowed his head and said, "*Introibo ad altare Dei.*" I had been brought by providential design to the Mass of All Time. At its close, I simply said to myself, "Now *that's* Catholic!" and never returned to the pathetic Roman protestant "shadow" rite.

How did I know I had found the Mass of All Time, the Mass of the Roman Rite? First and most obviously, the solemnity and the dignity evidenced everywhere in the ceremony of worship. This was not the raucous rumblings of the modern world brought indoors on Sunday to continue to amuse and to entertain. This was serious worship, unlike anything in the rest of the week, unlike anything to be found anywhere else in the world. This was uplifting, this was spiritual, this was God-centered, this was higher, nobler and richer than anything the world could offer. My intellect confirmed what my emotions first sensed—this was the Holy Sacrifice of the Mass, the Traditional Rite of Worship of the One, Holy, Catholic and Apostolic Roman Church.

The years have proven this judgment to be correct. This rite of worship indeed possesses the four marks of the True Church. It is ONE. From Sunday to Sunday, from priest to priest, from place to place, there is sameness to the rite. You do not find invention of detail or wholesale innovation as you find in the *Novus Ordo* Masses, where when you walk into the church you have no idea what to expect. The Traditional Mass possesses oneness and unity in its parts; it is a source of unending revelation and instruction. It possesses oneness and unity in its celebration, bringing together all the worship through sacrifice on the all the altars of the world to the greater glory of the One Triune God.

It is HOLY. The dignity, solemnity and nobility are obvious; they can perhaps be found in pale and puny imitation occasionally in the new rite. This is most obvious in the attitude and conduct of the priest. The priest in the Mass of All Time is an *alter Christus* and as such performs the Great Sacrifice in the person of Christ. If we all strive to have the old man decrease in us as Christ increases, the priest at the Mass has the fullness of Christ given to him as he re-enacts the sacrifice of Calvary. Everything points to God, present in the tabernacle on the altar; all moves toward the moment of sacrifice; all is majestic and sublime. This is not "Fr. Bob" regaling us, "GOOD MORNING! HOW ARE WE THIS MORNING?" followed by the latest excrescences of a tiny posturing imagination.

The holiness is inseparable from the ritual, and in the ritual, the personality of the individual must vanish. Some years ago, the great British director Tyrone Guthrie did a production of Sophocles' *Oedipus Rex* at the Stratford Festival in Ontario, Canada. He produced it as it would have been performed in Athens in the fifth century B.C. The actors wore long robes and masks, the speech emerged highly stylized and musical, the movement approached dance. This remarkable production recreated the ritual of the original Greek tragedy. When the production was filmed, the leading actor James Mason was unavailable because of another film obligation, so a Scottish actor named Douglas Campbell took over the role. Who could know? The masks hid the specific performer. This was theater as ritual, subsuming the particular to hint at higher, universal truths. Such, in a more exalted and spiritual way, is the ritual of the Mass of All Time. We should never be surprised that the result is an occasion of great holiness, nor should we be surprised that the new "shadow" sacrament, rooted as it is in the world and in its adoration of man above all else, should have dwindled to sad displays of ego and arrogance.

The Traditional Mass is CATHOLIC, the small "c" in catholic meaning universal. Because of its ritualistic nature and the uniformity of its structure, this Mass can travel the world without any need to bow to local custom. This universality is most obvious in the use of Latin, an old language, but hardly a dead language. A language, however, that is rarely used in day-to-day conversation and thus impervious to the inevitable vicissitudes of change found in commonly used languages. The sounds of the unusual words add to the solemnity; the precise meanings of the words remain unchanged and unchanging. For the holy time spent at the Mass, the punishment of the divided languages of man, a punishment for his arrogance in attempting to reach to heaven by building the Tower of Babel, is lifted and mankind through God's gift and Christ's sacrifice may know a moment of unity in speech. So one can travel around the world, as I have been fortunate enough to do, and find the same Mass celebrated in my parish church in Vienna, Virginia, or the jungles of Brazil, or the gorgeous historic structure of St. Nicolas du Chardonnet in Paris, or a hotel conference room in Cleveland or any of thousands of other places. The Mass of All Time is catholic, as well as Catholic.

The Traditional Mass is APOSTOLIC, handed down to us from the apostles, who received it from Our Lord Himself. The Holy Sacrifice of the Mass comes to us from Our Lord at the Last Supper and from Our Lord sacrificing Himself on the cross on

Calvary. The brilliant cross-cutting during the climactic scenes in Mel Gibson's *The Passion of the Christ* dramatically underlines this point. This was how God Himself told us we were to worship Him. So we should not be surprised that we can find portions of the Traditional Mass stretching back in time to the earliest days of the Church, the prayers of the Mass coming from the third century and from the sixth century, growing, developing, becoming more mysterious and sublime, but the ritual never changing in essence. How could it? We have an obligation to worship God as He commands us to worship Him. Through all of recorded history in the chronicles of the Old Testament that worship centered on blood sacrifice, all in preparation for the Great Sacrifice of Calvary. And down through the centuries that sacrifice continued, in unbloody form, through the Mass of the Ages, as God through His Church had commanded.

The *Novus Ordo* Mass is an aberration, a clear break with the worship of the Church throughout its past. Many commentators have made this clear, for example, famed liturgist Monsignor Klaus Gamber in his seminal work *The Reform of the Roman Liturgy*. The new order of worship, man-centered, innovational, worldly and unpredictable, the community meal on a table, has little organic connection with the Mass of All Time. How could it? In its origins, it was designed by a committee to provide a new rite that would be more ecumenical in nature and especially acceptable to Protestants, hence the approval given by six Protestant ministers before its release. Pope Paul VI in promulgating the new Mass struck at one of the two pillars of the Catholic Church. The Catholic Church rests on solid supports of Tradition and Scripture. Tradition precedes Scripture, for the apostles handed down many necessary elements of the faith before these essentials were set down in Scripture. The Church herself had existed for centuries before the body of approved Scripture was issued by the Council of Carthage in A.D. 397. In striking at the pillar of the Traditional Mass, Paul VI destroyed one of the two supports of Holy Mother Church. Can we be surprised the edifice has tottered and collapsed in subsequent years?

But a huge question remains. Is the *Novus Ordo* Mass pleasing to God? We know from scripture that not all sacrifice of worship is pleasing to God. In fact, some offerings He rejects and finds displeasing. We read in Genesis, Chapter 4: 3-7:

> And it came to pass after many days, that Cain offered, of the fruits of the earth, gifts to the Lord.
> Abel also offered of the firstlings of his flock, and of their fat: and the Lord had respect to Abel, and to his offerings.
> But to Cain and his offerings he had no respect: and Cain was exceedingly angry, and his countenance fell.
> And the Lord said to him: Why art thou angry? And why is thy countenance fallen?
> If thou do well, shalt thou not receive? But if ill, shall not sin forthwith be present at the door?...

God welcomed Abel's blood offering; He rejected Cain's "fruits of the earth," a phrase that appropriately but ominously appears in the *Novus Ordo* Mass. And who can doubt that in the years following its introduction, the Church now finds that "sin [is]...present at the door?" How can a Mass created by man, for man, in worship of man, be acceptable? How can the Mass of All Time handed down by apostolic tradition, the principal rite of worship for centuries, suddenly become an "extraordinary rite"? Only in a Wonderland world where "shadow" sacraments to please Protestants replace the real sacraments of the Catholic Church.

I returned to the church of my childhood recently for the first time in many years for the wedding of an old friend who was marrying late in life. The downstairs pews were overflowing and so I made my way to the balcony where there were a few remaining seats. As I looked down at the pulpit, I nearly fell over the rail. There, in front of the pulpit, in this liberal Protestant church, was the "table," the same table that has replaced the altar in so many Catholic churches. And, indeed, at one point in the wedding service the minister came to the table and went through a little service not unlike what is done at the *Novus Ordo* Mass. Nothing similar had ever been seen, or imagined, in my eighteen years of attending the church. But the true intent of the new Mass became that much clearer to me. Its point is ecumenical, the big lie that

Love in the Ruins

says differences need not divide us and that all religions can be friends and be one, worshipping the "one god." All I know is that is certainly not the Triune God.

In speaking to the "various Christian communities" at World Youth Day in Australia on July 18, 2008, Pope Benedict XVI stated that "a common Eucharist one day would only strengthen our resolve to love and serve one another...." So if the Congregationalists were friendly enough to accept our table, perhaps we could return the favor by learning from them. Open the Wonder bread and pour the Welsh's grape juice; however, as a Traditional Catholic, I will no longer wait around to hear the clink of glasses; I will go into the Church of the Triune God and rejoice when I hear the words "*Introibo ad altare Dei...*"

Dr. David Allen White taught World Literature at the Naval Academy in Annapolis, Maryland, for the better part of three decades. He taught many literature seminars at St. Thomas Aquinas Seminary in Winona, Minnesota. He is the author of *The Mouth of the Lion* and *The Horn of the Unicorn*.

Richard Cowden Guido

Day of the Locust

> There are two ways of getting home; and one of them is to stay there. The other is to walk round the whole world till we come back to the same place.
>
> –G. K. Chesterton, *The Everlasting Man*

Whatever else it is, the term "traditional" Catholic is certainly redundant; and regarding that, my particular tale of both staying home and walking around the world begins one evening, badly dating me I fear, with the reading of a Norman Mailer essay called *On Dread*.[1] The essay itself pilloried a poor fellow who clung to mysterious Christopher Hitchens-like superstitions in order to hide from real miracles, but the essay opened, and closed, with a haiku that went:

So soon to die
No sign of it is showing
Locust Cry

While a confident unbeliever when I began the essay, upon completing it I looked up to find an inescapable clarity in the room, and also knew I wasn't its source. I even shook my head to make it go away, but it didn't, and when it didn't, I both acknowledged what it was, and that it was expecting a response. Save for the intense clarity there was no especial emotion, but I remember finally addressing it, saying, probably silently: it will take a monumental effort of dishonesty to deny what is happening, which means that...You are. The next thought came easily: and since You are, then Christ must be Your...manifestation somehow.

---

[1] Norman Mailer, *The Presidential Papers* (New York: Putnam, 1963).

That conclusion was not especially surprising in that I had been raised a devout enough Protestant, when its suburban varieties were still pretty much Christologically orthodox, even morally so save for birth control. But my next unsolicited thought had no pedigree, in that though pre-Council Catholicism had a potent enough presence in my suburb, I'd never given its claims, nor any idea of ecclesia as such, any thought at all. In fact my grasp of Catholicism was little more than the contemporary slurs, and of course (though this dates me more than Norman Mailer does) that Catholics never ate meat on Friday. So as far as I can tell what followed was without preparation, something like direct instruction from the Clarity, which bade me think: if Christ is God, He would have left a Church.

Obvious enough in retrospect I suppose, but at the time it was sufficiently staggering for me now to take a facile pleasure in the irony by which I embraced it; for aloud I then said, "It's not the Salvation Army," my profession of faith, and I have been a Catholic since making it.

There were problems, however. In what I assume was some preliminary movement of grace, I had already found abortion repugnant on humanist grounds, and birth control on erotic ones, but there remained the dilemma of only knowing the Faith by virtue of such residue that Protestantism had afforded me in younger days. And of course there was the irritation of having to discover why it was all still true despite the Spanish Inquisition and such other dubious ecclesial adventures I was sure were out there, though I think I knew from the outset I should find, simply from pondering my own soul, that there would prove no small gulf between the Clarity *in se* that had visited me and His mix with the human effort to respond to it.

About which, I was also living with a woman at the time–I was twenty-one–and still far more entranced by the reality of God than by any obligations to that reality, a disjunction my confessors might yet consider unresolved. Even so, if without great solicitude for the "Thy Will" part, I began to pray the Our Father–*sans* the Protestant ending; I knew about that!–and had the decisive good fortune to know a man both eccentric and orthodox, a senior editor at the great old *Triumph* magazine in fact. Though I had always considered him a comedic if delightful anomaly, I now wrote outlining what had happened and asked him to come to New York to explain what I should do.

That he did, and though his instruction was subtle and rich, it can be boiled down to always invoking St. Rita of Cascia when money was needed—as I often did, and always got it—and despising such poseurs as Piltdown Pierre Teilhard. These excellent foundations have guided me since, though perusing an observation of Albert Camus back then doubtless augmented them: he wrote of a young man who studied the lives of the great to see how they died, but it is not the great who know how to die, Camus observed, rather old women in the hills of Italy. Locust cry, I was inclined to add.

All this as a prelude, but of a conversion based on no Catholic books, nor controversies, nor theological angst, nor anything I had remotely even considered theological reflection. Such things would come of course, but I didn't even attend my first Mass as a believer for another six months, though I have not stopped since that first. It was Paul VI's rite, but I knew nothing about that row either, save for an arguably instinctual Catholic sense even then that changing the Mass from Latin had been silly and wouldn't last.

Seven months later my *Triumph* mentor took me to Europe, wisely suspecting my new faith might not find much room to breathe in the homeland, as it certainly did in *Italia*, where a few artifacts from its human and divine glory remain riveting to those with eyes, and where I lived for most of the next decade. My affair (and final year at university) came to an end in these nascent months, if alas not my sins, but I recall vividly the many prayers of that time, mostly with saints and in particular St. Christopher, now my patron, both because he helped me get around and eventually overseas, but also in reactionary defiance to the rackets that pretended to deny both his place in heaven and abiding role on earth.

Love in the Ruins

Save for a few egregiously silly sermons, my recollection of the Masses I then attended is curiously misty, of a sort of banality before which I rested as humble learner, punctuated from all this by the Consecration. That miracle seemed no greater than that God–or you or I–should magically appear in a woman's womb, though it was not till later I read Pascal's query asking that if God created the heavens and the earth, where's the problem? It did not escape notice, however, given the phenomenon's quiet constancy, that the reality and adventures of the world must appear starkly different to those who recognized the miracle, against the more general consensi of those who don't.

And then I found myself in Rome, not ignoring its vivid and impossible *populi*, its wines and repasts, the sensual languor that pervades the Roman air, nor the cobblestone streets that accompany to splendor wherever one wanders. Not least midst the grandeur are its dazzling churches and what's in them of course, and while looking there I also sought intercession at the tombs of many saints, noticing as well numerous confessionals, making good use of them, I hope, over time. Not at first though, as I had not yet had specific instruction nor been formally received into the Church, yet if the Masses were Paul VI's, they were said reverently, often *ad orientem*, the churches were both ancient and Roman, and the *Italian* in which they were said was Latin enough for me.

I found work teaching English to Italians, the chief means by which I supported myself over those years, along with bit parts in films and better ones in theatre, a stint as a disc jockey and some writing; yet all that was but a compulsory backdrop to the serious business of sitting in cafes and reading the Russians, and Waugh, and Chesterton, and de Sales, and all the glories both canonical and obscure one could find. The death of a friend in the Tiber led me to leave Rome at one point for a few months of moody travel, but I finally got back, albeit with less than twenty dollars, and still fewer prospects. What followed were of course among my happiest months, an orange and a glass of milk a day, nights in a sleeping bag outside reading *Middlemarch*, and blissful meandering through

Rome's majesties and its churches, always in conversation with the saints and our God.

I was also taking instruction at the time, from then Fr. Wuerl, presently the U.S. capital's archbishop, and though he was satisfied I had already been sufficiently prepared by my mentor, long since back in the United States, the lunches Padre provided were more than a little welcome, as was his company. My saints' mirth eventually found me work at a Protestant orphanage on the outskirts of Rome; it provided a good sixty-five dollars a month, but also room and board, much fun with the kids, and still time to read and pray: and while living there I was conditionally baptized, and—appropriately in Rome—at the tomb of St. Peter received my first Holy Communion and the sacrament of Confirmation. The previous Christmas Padre Wuerl had invited me to a private Mass in the Basilica where, surprised to discover a Tridentine script at one of the altars, he offered it conceivably his final time in that rite; but though for me it was my first, another quarter century would pass before I would partake of another.

Of course one could perceive some sort of ecclesial crisis was in the air, yet apart from contempt for the prominent panderers like Hollywood Hans Kueng (and naughtily rooting for Lefebvre), in Rome I paid but cursory attention to either theological or ecclesial politics. It's true that practicing the Faith needs a bit of work and accepting it evades definitional category, but its teaching seemed, and yet does, elusive only to those determined to find it so, or who don't bother. So though omniscience and free will agitated me for a tad once, until I applied Pascal's gambit to it, the enemy's capture of institutional levers in the Church troubled my own faith no more than it disturbed the inelusive truths. One perhaps unsettling example of this struck me with some force during my first of three trips to Lourdes, where I noticed that if love is not an option, but an obligation, the option of hell must necessarily follow.

Thus years passed, not unhappy, if occasionally problematic ones, income improved, declined, improved again, the cafes held stable, the prayers stable enough, until eventually I undertook a postulancy with the Friars Minor in Spoleto. While I was there Paul VI died, and then, during a novitiate at San Damiano in St. Francis's Assisi, I first saw John Paul II during his Pontificate's early pilgrimage to where *Italia*'s patron had once lived. I may have had a religious vocation–though not to the priesthood, I knew–but if so, I fled it just before first vows, exploring the Franciscans further in New York and California, yet as the former were not recognizably Catholic and the latter only barely so, I came to understand that the real decision had been made in the land where my faith had taken root.

Thirty years old then, I came back to settle in its embryo of New York. While the ecclesiastical crisis came more into focus there, I was confident the new Pope would bring it to heel, though the hostility of the world–and its faux Catholic minions–was no less plain now than it had been since Bethlehem. Accordingly I began to fight against the abortion horror, first as a volunteer, then as a spy, taking polls for the Democrats, from which I passed information to the pro-life folks who used it, such as it was, to help win a close upset Senate victory the year of the Reagan sweep.

And I kept at it, though in those heady Reagan (and Wojtyla) days, I also began to notice something of the central role Catholic institutional apparats played in upholding the abortion trade, on occasion directly, but rather more in protecting, and promoting, such moral corruption as can thrive only on murder–and just how central struck home upon reading of the New Jersey legislature's struggle with a sex ed course for its public schools. Designed by a man whose own efforts had obliged students first to draw pictures of their parents in sexual intimacy and then tell the instructor whether doing so made them "horny," the legislators were prepared to reject the depravity until an energetic intervention by Newark Archbishop Peter Gerety (and his fellow Jersey bishops) got the–mandatory–thing passed after all. A review of the sex ed courses in Jersey's parochial schools revealed instruction no less inimical to common decency, or to the Catholic faith, so that for me an obvious epiphany took hold: the slaughter of innocents neither would stop, nor could, unless Catholics recovered their episcopacy and their Church.

As it proved, even back in Rome I'd done my first Catholic piece where with bohemian mien I'd meet with various faux Catholics to join me in denouncing the Faith and all it stood for, which enthusiasms I then passed to my mentor—now my godfather—who dutifully published them in a notoriously orthodox weekly for which he worked, called *The Wanderer*. Still scruffy enough in my thirties, I began to employ the same method here for various publications, eventually settling with *The Wanderer* itself, still notorious, as its New York correspondent; and where its readers learned not only how powerful in her institutions had the Church's enemies become, but also how intensely they loathed both the Catholic Faith and those who hold it.

These vigorous days seemed of some value: during them, Clergy Prefect Cardinal Oddi told me proponents of contraception were "out of the Church"; Cardinal Gagnon gave specific instructions on how to battle frauds like Rembert Weakland and Joe Bernardin, the latter of whom was kind enough to denounce me personally to Secretary of State Casaroli; more than one bishops' conference gathering took the time to lie about *The Wanderer's* "misinformation to Rome" as a *Newsweek* story's article titled it; Reagan's Mexico City policy survived, James Baker grumbled to an ally of mine, because our *Wanderer* editorial urged Catholics not to support Reagan in '84 if it didn't; and poor Mario Cuomo charged me with being responsible for "the worst moment of [his] life" because during the first press conference as New York Archbishop, Cardinal O'Connor left open the possibility when I asked if "Archbishops still had the authority, as in St. Ambrose's day, to excommunicate Catholic heads of state when they are responsible, as Theodosius was and Governor Cuomo is, for the slaughter of innocents." As to Peter Gerety there was also "The Newark Chronicles," an eighteen-part series that exposed the ferocity by which he and so many like him had used their office to attack Catholics and their faith whenever and however it could be done.

Love in the Ruins

It seemed I might have found my vocation after all, though a deeper one had already taken hold upon an Italian-born beauty winning my heart at an opera, and upon my winning hers. Before marrying, we first returned to her small (and magnificent) Calabrese town for a formal betrothal ceremony, wherein the priest transported me to the Middle Ages upon holding, along with admonitions to love and fidelity, that our coming across the ocean was a stern example to the townsfolk they were to attend his church, and not the one down the road.

In New York we were married also in an Italian church where Mother Cabrini had once been a parishioner, and where St. Rita's statue and others like hers held sway. It was a large and lovely church, not ill-attended, the Scalabrini priests were orthodox, gave properly admonitory absolutions, and though they faced the congregation, said Paul VI's Mass with reverence; so that as the battles for truth and justice raged outside, as did the joys and tribulations common to our lot, not a few were the moments of solace, sometimes more, that my prayers knew midst those statues.

The battles, nonetheless, did continue, and not wholly without cause for hope on the Catholic side. During Reagan's re-election campaign, O'Connor not only defanged determined efforts by Bernardin and his conference bureaucrats to minimize the unborn, he did so in a manner that went beyond electoral politics, even beyond abortion, in that he seemed clearly, and finally, to be challenging the faux "spirit" of Vatican II. Most practicing Catholics still believed, or at least hoped, in the promise of that Council, and with Wojtyla at the helm and O'Connor his manifest voice in this country, that promise seemed at last ready to take root here. When His Holiness then announced an Extraordinary Synod for the twentieth anniversary of the Council's end, the Catholics were convinced, and their enemies feared, that a definitive restoration was at hand.

With that confidence I returned to Rome to cover and write a book[2] about it, and was not unhappy with the plaudits and de-

---

[2] Richard Cowden Guido, *John-Paul II & the Battle for Vatican II* (Trinity Publications, 1986).

nunciations the opus provoked, nor entirely with the Synod itself. Indeed in the year following it, preparations for a new catechism were announced, my old friend Fr. Wuerl was sent as a coadjutor to quell a bishop's nonsense in Seattle, Peter Gerety was forced to retire early, Cardinal Ratzinger kept issuing vivid statements and documents, a priest named Curran was stripped of any Catholic right to claim theological expertise, and not least Reagan's Supreme Court appointments seemed to have put *Roe v. Wade* on the ropes. Yet despite all this and more, I was not alone in a growing uneasiness that, for all the hoopla, not much in the ecclesiastical establishment was really changing. That people hostile to the Faith were manifestly still in charge was monstrous enough, but what began to appear inescapable after the Synod was what had in fact been the prime quandary right along since Vatican II, and indeed during it: that those clerics who still were Catholic, not excluding the Bishops of Rome, had apparently decided it better, or in any event tolerable, to mollify the predators rather than to defend the faithful.

The gloom deepened when four pro-life referenda went down to defeat in the '86 midterm elections that also saw pro-abortion politicians win back a majority in the U.S. Senate; but it was also then that I began to notice a remarkable Catholic development in the country, with Protestants too, that would soon challenge the abortion culture as nothing ever had or, in a way, could. It began, for me, when among the different stories I collected for the weekly articles and now column I wrote, one was about a young woman who'd passively intervened at a Florida abortion mill and sought to dissuade mothers there from turning their children over to abortionist mercy. I had been vaguely aware of her and that "rescues," as they were called, had been taking place around the country, the first having been organized by *Triumph* editor and Goldwater's *Conscience of a Conservative* ghostwriter Brent Bozell; but upon looking more closely at the one in Florida, the implications of it were immediately stunning.

The woman's name was Joan Andrews, and after her conviction by a judge in a non-jury trial, he sought a promise that she wouldn't rescue again and, when she refused, denied bail, whereupon Andrews replied that "the only way I can protest for unborn children now is by non-cooperation in jail." She accordingly went limp in the courtroom and prison, for which she was further punished with solitary confinement and denial of the right to attend Mass, but still didn't relent, so that when they dragged her back four months later for sentencing, the judge was imperfectly pleased. Three others who had been arrested with Andrews had meanwhile agreed to the judge's demands and been released, and though later in the day he would sentence two men convicted of accessory to murder to four years, in Andrews's case he ignored the Florida guidelines that recommended a year; and upon observing that prison officials have "their ways" of ensuring cooperation, sentenced her to a maximum five.

However vicious, the "ways" failed nonetheless in their object, and though on any day Andrews could have been released from solitary by agreeing to cooperate in jail, or from jail altogether by agreeing not to rescue, she continued to refuse both and thereby absorbed some measure of the injustice to the unborn by instead languishing throughout 1987 essentially unknown, and alone, in a Florida maximum security cell. People finally began to notice. I too started writing about her that year, eventually collecting her letters for a kind of biography;[3] but for me, as for many, it would prove more than just a story, as there was about her, and her witness, and her words, a quality too compelling to be satisfied with but admiration.

And so as I wrote, I also began to rescue, to enter the death-camps so that before any children could be killed in them, it would first be necessary to drag me, and others—eventually tens of thousands—from the place where their murder had been scheduled. Over the next four years I thus intervened some fifty times, spent something like a year altogether in jail, and in so doing came to understand that, crucial as were the many lives in consequence saved, no less crucial were the beatings and prison and injustice

---

[3] Richard Cowden Guido, *You Reject Them, You Reject Me: The Prison Letters of Joan Andrews* (Trinity Publications, 1988).

the rescuers were willing to endure, because by accepting all that, we were also able to stand with the kids who had not been saved. Dostoevski says somewhere that the chief characteristic of love is willingness to suffer on behalf of the beloved, which is of course what Christ did for each of us; and in their effort to imitate that example did the rescuers seek to love, even those killed, for as long as the rescues and the witness continued.

The history books won't mention it,[4] but Operation Rescue as it came to be called, in terms of incidents and arrests, provoked the most massive civil resistance in American history. Without exception, on the part of the rescuers, and indeed by definition, their rescues were non-violent; but in the end they couldn't endure, or anyhow didn't, in that given the central role abortion had taken in the social polity, rescue would have had to unearth people ready to devote their entire lives to it: to the paradoxical Catholic idea of giving up everything they are entitled to pursue precisely in order to affirm the value of that pursuit. In effect, a religious vocation, not unlike the Mercedarians, who in the Middle Ages turned themselves over by the thousands to be slaves in order to ransom other men home. Finding comparable men and women in this age would have demanded, as in the earlier one, some larger apparatus of moral and other support that this time didn't materialize, even after years of at least one but usually dozens of rescues every week and many rescuers in jail, with often tremendous courage from people not especially disposed to it. The rescues accordingly slowed, eventually dried up almost entirely, and when in despair some people then started shooting abortionists, the country's most widespread civil resistance in our history came to an end.

My own first rescue was on Good Friday in 1987, my last in July of '91, and in those years I devoted my life almost entirely to its organization and execution. When it died, I toyed, not seriously I suppose, with undertaking some witness alone, like Joan Andrews's; yet apart from the likelihood this was but entirely a de-

---

[4] *A History of Operation Rescue: 1970-1990* is the most accurate account, but available only in manuscript.

lusion, there was a humility and even holiness about Joan I knew eluded my own soul, not to say how fair such a thing would be to my Italian bride.

She, in fact, had not merely stood with me through it all, but had herself rescued and been jailed many times, so that when after ten years of exquisite happiness together, albeit childless, God finally granted us the miracle of our son, the other possibility was put aside, for good no doubt.

Since it was, and though God's goodness and creation delighted my soul no less, a certain gloom also returned. The slaughter of the unborn and all that upheld it proceeded apace, and after years of effort fighting it I felt in the moment, and was, decisively defeated. Personal mercies remained abundant, evident, in my bride and son especially, but in many other ways too, and not least that she landed work for an explicitly Catholic outfit devoted to pregnant women with no place to go, and even run by a rescuer: and through which in consequence there are not impossibly hundreds of children alive today who would not have been but for her efforts, which continue as I write. There was also this, that though by any human measure the worldly defeat of Christ on Good Friday seemed complete, my gloom recalled a more salient dimension to that defeat; as it did that in the lives of saints, I suspect without exception, worldly failure proved the means by which genuine sanctity finally found room to breathe.

Our son Athanasius was baptized in the old Italian church, and there was nothing especially wrong with the new priest who shortly afterward replaced the one who'd baptized the boy; but though my faith was undimmed, Pope Paul's new form of Mass, which in the strength of my youth had carried it, seemed worse than just inadequate to this dark wood of defeat in mid age. I had never really much thought about the liturgy until then, or rather until we discovered near our home an Armenian-Rite Mass, Catholic of course, a sort of hybrid of both Byzantine and Tridentine, if more the latter; but its mystery and reverence and beauty did more than just carry me in those days, as Paul's Mass no longer could.

In the joy of Rome and discovery, and the battles that followed in New York, I had always assumed the problems with Paul's Mass were in the nature of its execution and the unbelieving priests who sought enthusiastically to desecrate it; but in the quiet wonder of a Mass entirely formed, not to entertain, but to adore, it became impossible to ignore how central such adoration was—to everything. Not always sufficient no doubt, as is true in so many theological realms, but still necessary, or so my walk around the world has led me to conclude.

As the Armenian church was large, but with exceptions sparsely attended, I allowed my toddling son to wander and wriggle through most of the Mass, save at the Consecration by which all else that does, can thrive. That changed when a St. Peter Fraternity school hired me as its headmaster and the boy attended first grade there, where he would receive his first Holy Communion. Though we had doubtless attended some Tridentine Masses in those years, at the school we did so all but daily; and in the reverence of the larger congregation there, so did his own reverence take hold. Later, when he transferred to a Ukrainian school nearer home, he went daily with his mother to the Byzantine rite there; and thus our eclectic liturgical prayer abides, at Masses where adoration is the alpha, and the omega too.

Sometimes, for funerals or baptisms, on occasion just sloth, I still attend Masses designed apparently by a fellow named Bugnini[5] for motives that seem too painfully to have been realized. Even so, I make a point of receiving at least annually at these, in union with my fellows toward that mutual effort to get home, though I never attend Masses where there are girls on the altar, I should perhaps note. By the time that got authorized, I had long since drifted from Paul's rite, and again had never given much thought to the matter, save knowing it an initiative from Church enemies. Once formalized, however, its perversion was

---

[5] Archbishop Annibale Bugnini, now dead, is considered the chief architect of Paul's Mass; and if not conclusive, there is yet substantial evidence indicating his private adherence to Freemasonry, which has long, and openly, expressed hope to see the Catholic Faith destroyed.

plain, an embrace against the Faith of this age's conviction that women are in themselves but a deformity, whose hope lies only in learning to do the things men do, and so become like them, and be whole.

The clerical homosexual and rape atrocities were finally soon after exposed, the abortion holocaust thrived on, with now a growing movement to make even verbal opposition to it some kind of hate crime, and of course the demographics of Europe are such that had only another Black Plague struck in 1962, instead of Vatican II, the population of that continent would be far larger than it now is. Pope Benedict XVI has meanwhile formally stated the obvious about the legitimacy of the Tridentine rite, but his call to make it available, like his predecessor's, remains ignored and successfully resisted; and Church institutions also remain comprehensively in the hands of Her enemies.

It is hard to avoid recognizing a correlation between this epoch's nihilism and even the believing bishops' failure to read it, or counter it, at and since Vatican II; nor to see that if the effort to thank God is not founded and expressed in adoration, men are likely to drift, as they have, into the despair that characterizes this era. Perhaps fair again to observe, that the slaughter of innocents, the other horrors upon us, will not abate until Catholics recover their episcopacy and their Church; and that when they do, the rite of Paul VI will fade from the altar into history.

As the social polity and fabric meanwhile unravel, God's creation and goodness stand no less resplendent in its midst, indeed, as ever, the dramatic alternative to it, as do His truths. That ought to be enough of course, but as man's will and mind, and so soul, get so easily fogged, he could perhaps do worse than to restore some clarity to the point, quietly, perhaps best at a Mass that sees its source, and adores it; until the locust cries.

Richard Cowden Guido is the author of several history books, including *John-Paul II and the Battle for Vatican II*.

Dr. John C. Rao

From Hoboken to Eternity

The Value of Catholic Traditionalism in the Life of One Traditionalist

It was in the Hoboken Train Station, waiting to return to Drew University after a day in Manhattan, that a powerful intellectual and spiritual freight engine bearing "every good and perfect gift" barreled directly into me. One of my professors, the late and sorely lamented James Lo Gerfo, had insisted upon a reading of St. Augustine's *Confessions* for his course on Early Medieval History. There I stood, under the departure announcement board, doing my routine academic duty, perfunctorily underlining some of Augustine's meditations, when a stray thought took possession of my mind, heart, and soul: what if these words were meant for my life instead of being meant just for my grade this semester?

That idea, quite frankly, made me sick to my stomach. Familiar knots from previous life-changing moments began to form again. Remembering their painfulness, but helpless to untie them and "return to normalcy," I took the first opportunity to run to the professor responsible for my condition and explain to him my discomfort. He then made certain that the journey that had begun in Hoboken did not end for me only at Drew.

It was at Drew that I also gained the invaluable guidance of James Pain, a Methodist cleric and Chairman of the Religion Department. Dr. Pain had a profound interest in the search for God and a scholar's rigor in teaching the history of Christian belief and practice. Not only did he introduce me to a systematic study of Roman Catholic doctrine unmarred by dubious "signs of the time" and irrational swooning over the mysteries of the Omega Point. He also organized the semester abroad at Oxford in 1972 which led to my sojourn in that blessed environment for five further years of doctoral work. Even more importantly for this little essay, it was Dr. Pain who, during that first semester abroad, assigned me a paper on religious life in Britain. This brought me to a Tridentine Mass at Westminster Cathedral, an idle question to a member of the congregation regarding who could best inform me about current conditions of the Catholic Church in England, and the beginning of my thirty-two-year friendship with one of the greatest lay heroes of our time, the late Michael Davies.

But I am now getting far ahead of my story. So much more had already happened before that meeting with Michael in his suburban London house, all of which prepared me to appreciate what it was he had to say, about painful developments in the liturgy in particular. For in the months after my Hoboken experience, Professor Lo Gerfo had introduced me to two institutions which were to be central to my further spiritual and intellectual formation.

One of these was the two-year old Roman Forum, created in 1968 to defend Pope Paul VI's encyclical letter *Humanae Vitae*, and offering monthly lectures by Drs. Dietrich von Hildebrand and William Marra at a packed Keating Hall on Fordham University's Rose Hill Campus. The other was the Intercollegiate Studies Institute, whose summer schools provided access to the teaching of an extremely wide range of conservative academics, including those espousing the rich political and social thought of the European Catholic Right. Exposure to these organizations meant that I was present when von Hildebrand electrified the audience in the Bronx with his fervent call for a determined petitioning of Rome for the restoration of the "old Mass." It also meant that I heard Dr. Thomas Molnar, one of the most lucid and courageous of the ISI speakers, when he hammered at the dangers coming from the school of Leo Strauss and the first appearance in American rightist circles of what no one yet knew would some day dominate it under the name of "neo-conservatism."

Those years after 1970 were exciting ones indeed, and the reason for the excitement was the fact that I found myself in the middle of the budding Catholic Traditionalist Movement. Discovery and embrace of that Movement had come without my looking for it or expecting it, through personal confusion and happy accident alone. Nevertheless, it proved itself to be of central importance to the shaping of my life and the confirmation of my Faith—all of which indicates to me that I was led to Traditionalism through God's Providence.

Traditionalism proved its superabundant worth to me in four ways over the following decades, to begin with by teaching me the difference between a serious, open-minded, joyful intellectual endeavor on the one hand, and illogical, nostalgic, willful, and closed-minded ventures on the other. My introduction to the movement came through the influence of an eclectic mixture of Platonists and Thomists, with the Platonists, like Dietrich von Hildebrand and William Marra, in the ascendant.

These men were not *Neo-Platonists* espousing some gnostic vision of contact with ever-greater corruption the further down on the Great Chain of Being from spiritual to material life one descended. Rather, they were Christian Platonists in love with God and man, emphasizing the goodness of Creation and the immense sorrow of the Fall. Most importantly, they were devout men who called attention to the supernatural light penetrating into every part of nature through the Incarnation, and the glorious role each of nature's elements, from the lowest to the highest, was called upon to play in the divine plan of "transformation of all things in Christ."

Such a teaching, fed in the years to come by a reading of works like Fr. Emile Mersch's *The Whole Christ* and Werner Jaeger's study of *Greek Paideia*, showed me that nothing was superfluous to the task of raising the individual to God; that one needed solid theological, philosophical, political, economic, and aesthetic cooperation with supernatural grace, *all in the context of authoritative social life*, beginning with the family and moving upwards in order to get anywhere in this most exalted of enterprises; that an openness to a sifting through all that nature had offered—and might in new ways offer in the future—was required by men and women who *really* believed in the Incarnation and its consequences; and that this had to be done under acceptance of one supreme condition: that one's eyes remained focused firmly on the Christ responsible for such bounty, and on that same Christ continued in His Mystical Body, the Church.

Hence the importance of the Traditional Mass, which von Hildebrand's books, such as *Liturgy and Personality*, made so wonderfully clear. Here one had the supreme "tool" for sanctification, with everything supernatural and natural ordered according to the proper hierarchy of values, beginning with the fact that it was aimed *primarily* at the worship of God, from which all things useful to mankind—all tools—only *secondarily* flow. All had its place in such worship—simplicity and grandeur, silence and public acclamation, humble recognition of unworthiness and rejoicing in superabundant love of the Almighty—in a dramatic and aesthetically brilliant presentation of man's relationship with his Creator appealing simultaneously to eyes, ears, senses, mind, heart, and soul.

Tampering with such magnificence, under the guidance of a spirit that put the secondary teaching function of the Mass—and, hence, the service of man—above the truly overriding consideration of what most fittingly adores the Godhead, was thus the most certain means of failing to achieve *both* purposes: that of praising what is above and instructing what is below. The more I understood this, the more the unfolding liturgical nightmare in the Roman Church became unbearable to me.

Luckily, my courses with Dr. Pain back at Drew had drawn my attention to the many Eastern Catholic Churches of the New York metropolitan area and the possibility of living the solid, Incarnation-drunk liturgical life stolen from me by a misguided "reform." Before I knew it, I was singing the Liturgy of St. John Chrysostom myself, and bringing my favorite Ruthenian priest to Drew to expose others to its beauty.

Still, the years after 1970 acquainted me with two contrasting, closed-minded approaches to wisdom as well—one that was primarily illogical and nostalgic, and the other determinedly willful in spirit. The first became ever more noticeable as Catholic

Traditionalism and Conservatism parted their ways; the other through wrenching daily contact with the "mainstream" Church and the development of its understanding of "renewal."

Dietrich von Hildebrand had begun the Roman Forum in union with the Catholic weekly newspaper *The Wanderer* and in conjunction with the creation of Catholics United for the Faith. This alliance was broken due to von Hildebrand's insistence on the need to criticize not the validity but the failings and inferiority of the *Novus Ordo* in relation to the traditional rite of Mass. His former partners, Conservatives as opposed to Traditionalists, believed that loyal, orthodox Catholics were obliged to defend the reform of the liturgy, and did so, often enthusiastically. In the process, they accepted more and more changes that they themselves had bitterly fought when the revolution began.

It struck me that the conservatives' attitude concerning contemporary issues was in open and illogical battle with the historical traditions and saintly lives that they continued to praise...and which I honestly think, in their heart of hearts, they continued to prefer. Conservative grasping at bits and pieces of the ancient heritage—a Kyrie sung in Latin here, an old hymn there—in the midst of the general debacle seemed to me to "miss the point" and reflect precisely that "nostalgic" mentality that our common progressive enemies wrongly accused the Traditionalists of nurturing. Traditionalist concern was never for Latin or one specific gesture or another in the Offertory as such; it was a concern for *an organic liturgical whole aimed primarily at the adoration of God*. Everything cherished outside of that whole was, at best, a pious nostalgia; something akin to a warm memory of a top hat, still worn with remembered pride, but now together with a new and absurd uniform of torn jeans and platform shoes. And this same illogical, nostalgic spirit seemed to reign everywhere that conservative Catholics of varied types congregated.

Willfulness was to be found in the "mainstream," expressed by the progressive ideologues choreographing the *danse macabre* that Catholic life in the 1970's had become. I simply found no means of engaging a discussion with Whirling Dervishes in the grip of renewal fever. All of their man-centered activities were defended by them with reference to the obvious guidance of a Holy Spirit whom I was said to despise, a Holy Spirit who had suddenly and inexplicably exchanged His friendship for Catholic Tradition for a Shiva-like passion for its annihilation. Mockery and distortion of Traditionalist arguments were the unchanging weapons in the progressive arsenal in those days, one favorite being the response to my justification for the old liturgy with the claim that I should then want my sermons to be delivered in Latin as well. Theirs was not the path of victory through rational discourse; progressives had passionately embraced the road reflected in *Triumph of the Will*. There is only one Spirit, and the Zeitgeist interpreted by us is His Prophet! That was their mantra.

As far as I was concerned, the only thing solidly intellectual and rationally useful that came out of my contact with the forces of renewal was the growth of my own library. For the Holy Spirit apparently directed church after church, priest after priest, seminary after seminary, literally to toss into the rubbish bin beautiful altar missals, breviaries, copies of the Church Fathers, and major theological, philosophical, and historical treatises. They certainly were following a precedent started in the Age of Reason in doing this. After all, the eighteenth-century Enlightened Absolutist Joseph II of Austria filled the foundations of state buildings due to a similar spirit of Spring Cleaning, loading them up with the precious texts of suppressed Jesuit libraries. In any case, I scavenged the rubbish bins and swelled my shelves with all the discarded nonsense of nearly two millennia.

My "Incarnation-drunk" Platonist teachers had also taught me the crucial importance of examining the whole of the historical record, sacred and profane, in order to understand how Catholics had sifted the good from the bad in nature in past ages and learn which paths to follow and which pitfalls to avoid in the future. It was through his knowledge of the historical sources—in this case, the First Vatican Council and its aftermath—that von Hildebrand was aware of the validity of his own nuanced position. Examination of the sources made it crystal clear that the Pope had the authority to impose the changed liturgy on the Church, and we Catholics the duty to recognize its validity. On the other hand, it just as firmly showed that believers also had the right and the responsibility to criticize this action and beg that it be recognized as a mistake and overturned when convinced of its dangers.

By now, I was deeply interested in exactly how the Church had managed to get itself in the mess that I saw poisoning all around me, and what it was that the faithful had done to emerge from similar crises in the past. Therefore, I set to work in Oxford on a doctoral dissertation that might satisfy my curiosity and enable me to contribute to the Traditionalist Movement in days to come. Step by step, this led me to a study of Catholic reactions to the Enlightenment, the problem of Naturalism, and the ravages of the French Revolution. It also brought me to investigate that deep fountain of lay and clerical interest in the Incarnation and its consequences that burst forth after 1848, feeding the Syllabus of Errors and Catholic Social Teaching, and providing the waters of Catholic speculation from which von Hildebrand himself had drunk. Step by step, this also pulled me towards my second, totally unexpected example of the importance of the message taught by the Catholic Traditionalist Movement: its effectiveness in showing how to deal with the reality of the devil.

When I finally found the theme for my doctoral dissertation, I was happily ensconced at St. Edmund Hall in Oxford. I lived in a room on Longwall Street overlooking the Deer Park at Magdalen College, and had worked out a routine that seemed destined to make me into the perfect Renaissance man. I labored each day at the Bodleian Library, took my exercise on Christ Church Meadow, enjoyed drinks and dinner with my friends in historic pubs, listened to the opera and committed the arias to memory before retiring for the night. Lent of 1975 was approaching, and I planned to cap my Florentine routine with a season of penitence that would enable me to enjoy the Easter Feast appropriately. And then a crisis hit, an existential crisis of the sort that I had read about in Kierkegaard but never prepared for facing myself. As with the experience in Hoboken, this began with a sudden thought taking possession of me. The thought this time was of a saint who died and discovered...nothing. More specifically, it was the thought of a saint who could not even really discover nothing because of the total end of his consciousness that came with his demise. In short, I was seized with the fear that there was no God; that I had come from nowhere and was headed for nowhere. If this were true, if the Faith were vain, it was not just heaven that would be lost. There could be no enjoyment in even the simplest act of living here on earth. If eating, drinking, and being merry were not connected with a final supernatural purpose, none of them had the slightest significance whatsoever.

This was the most miserable experience that I have ever had to date. I was paralyzed, and the paralysis lasted quite some time, mitigated only by two lifelines. One was a mechanical commitment to continuing my doctoral work that allowed me to escape from confronting the vision of absolute nothingness for eight hours each day. The other was the inexplicable realization that every time I actually consulted my Reason, this never failed to lead me to the conclusion that there was indeed a God, and that if there were a God, that Catholicism in and of itself was worthy of the act of Faith I had once made in it. I could not escape the conclusion that my problem was that I could not bring myself to believe what my Reason repeatedly told me to be true. I needed to find a way to *believe* what I *knew*, and then proceed from that *knowledge* back into my *faith*.

Three friends–Dietrich Warns, a fellow student from Germany, a good Franciscan priest whose name I never learned, and Dr. William Marra's wife Marcelle–finally showed me the way out of this abominable Black Hole. All of them insisted that I had come face to face with the devil, and the only thing that could effectively fight his call to *nothingness* was...*everything*. Everything around me, all of which was indeed real, was, they argued, continually speaking to me in varied ways of aspects of the message of Truth, Goodness, and Beauty that my *Reason* was willing to accept and pull upwards towards the thought of God. Everything around me was important to my spiritual cure, and nothing could be considered superfluous to it. I had now only to use this natural bounty on behalf of Faith.

After struggling with this advice for a while, I realized that these friends were reinforcing exactly what I had learned in the Traditionalist Movement from the very outset: that Christ's Incarnation confirms the value of God's Creation; that all of nature is a powerful aid in the raising of the mind and soul to a desire for the supernatural, and that all of nature transformed in Christ was of an even greater—an infinitely greater—assistance.

So I dived back into the fullness of Christ both through all that could in some manner be connected with Him, as well as all that He was in and of Himself: the beauty of Oxford, Europe, and Catholic culture as a whole; the wonders of the intellectual life; the warmth of friendship with others seeking the Truth; prayer; the life of an age-old liturgy which, through the Eastern Catholics and the English Indult, was mercifully available to me and provided me my daily spiritual food. When I had regained my Faith, I regained the conviction of the value of my Reason. When I regained my Reason, I regained Reason's aid in confirming my Faith. And my Faith and Reason together warned me never again to abandon that message of the Incarnation and its consequences that Catholic Traditionalism *alone* had taught me to study and nurture, never again to abandon all the tools that had been shown historically to push men into the arms of Christ and keep them there.

By 1978, with my doctorate finished and my sense of how Catholics had fallen into their current predicament deepened, Oxford had become more dear to me than life itself. This, in itself, would have made my departure for anywhere quite difficult. Nevertheless, my return to the United States became particularly unpleasant when I began experiencing problems not only in explaining what I had learned, but even in merely beginning a conversation about the life-and-death contrast of an Incarnation-minded Catholicism with a naturalist worldview in the first place. Most painful of all was the fact that this difficulty was proving to be true with many Traditionalists as well as Conservatives and progressive ideologues, not to speak of colleagues, high school friends, and family members. Horrible to recount, I found that the same trouble was manifesting itself with each subsequent summer return to Europe and contact with Europeans outside my rather rarefied circle of former Oxford comrades. Chance (or Providence) guided me to an explanation for this phenomenon, and this explanation, which came through the Traditionalist Movement, confirmed the value of Catholic Traditionalism for me yet a third time.

As soon as I returned from Oxford, Dr. Marra had begun to call upon my services as lecturer at the Roman Forum. One day, he commissioned a topic for a talk concerned with problems at Catholic University. As I developed this, it transmuted into a study of the Americanist Crisis in the Church in the United States at the turn of the twentieth century. Confrontation of Americanism with the critique of its character that I found, once again, in the Incarnation-based thinkers to which the Traditionalist Movement had directed my attention was startling. It unveiled the peculiar nature of the anti-intellectual, materialist, "pragmatic," but non-violent and seemingly "friendly" way in which the Enlightenment had made its progress in both Britain and the United States...to the most effective detriment of the Catholic cause known to history.

My study of Americanism helped to open my eyes to the explanation of many things: why my elementary and high school education had aimed me away from any serious investigation of the questions most important to life in general and towards mindless, materialist goals; why "pointless" intellectual discussions were generally avoided by American society; why both Faith and Reason failed to have a social impact; how a naturalist and revolutionary principle could find a way to masquerade as a solid bulwark of Tradition and the essence of patriotism; how "pragmatism" and the need to avoid "divisiveness" were used to prevent people from finding their way out of a spiritual dead end back to Catholic sanity; how a Europe fearful that opposition to an American-inspired Pluralism would be construed as sympathy for Nazism and Communism or simply outright insanity was won for the cause of

Dr. John C. Rao

mindlessness. Walter Matt, the founding editor of *The Remnant*, was so eager that I continue with the critique of Americanism that this lecture had begun that he insisted I publish a brochure on the subject; hence the start of what is now a regular collaboration with that journal. "Everybody in the world is infected with this Americanist virus," Dr. Marra told me. "Your life's work has been laid out. I don't envy you."

Such foreboding predictions proved to be miserably accurate, especially with respect to the strong hint of possible frustrations in my work. Filled with missionary zeal, I managed to intrigue a rather wide range of people and organizations, thus obtaining invitations to speak almost everywhere…once. After that, oversized *persona non grata* mats were laid at many a formerly friendly door. Bit by bit, the invitations degenerated from microphones at elegant Opus Dei parlors with wine and cheese receptions to those at suburban firehouses and out-of-the-way catering halls with snacks of stale donuts and bad coffee.

Perhaps the most depressing aspect of this labor was the fact that Catholic Traditionalists themselves were often among the least responsive to my arguments. Rather than being willing to listen to proofs that Americanism and Pluralism were the most effective tools for leading them into acceptance of the Enlightenment naturalism that lay behind our contemporary crisis, liturgical as well as theological, they often waved me away as a dangerously treasonous kook. Instead, they took refuge in explanations striking at one or the other head of the revolutionary hydra that had affected them personally, while neglecting the fact that they were frequently cooperating with other manifestations of that very same beast. Separation from the mainstream of life, while totally understandable, seemed to me to be making Traditionalists stranger and sadder rather than wiser; hence the influence of those who thought that they could deal with the disaster by acting like Protestant atomists in little houses on the prairie; of other, Rousseau-like anarchists committed to "unschooling" their children; of pseudo-fascists speaking of *Triumph of the Will* and blaring out hard rock on car radios while claiming to be militants determined to crush the menace of liberal theology. Meanwhile, despite what one can now in retrospect perceive, hopes for official Church support for the revival of the Traditional Mass appeared to be ever more groundless as the '70's turned to the '80's. "The movement," as one friend said, "is stationary."

By the mid-1980's, along with my closest, equally distressed collaborator, I began to wake up each morning thinking I was dead and in hell. People my age in New York City were beginning to make Big Time Bucks, buy beautiful apartments, and get boxes at the Opera. They would shout hello to me from their limousines while I sat on my tenement stoop drinking jug wine and listening to fading, crackling, spliced tapes of *Don Giovanni*. Traditionalists were losers and I was one of them. Tradition, above all else, was supposed to be tied in with a normal human life. What was normal about the way that I was living? Surely, it was time for a return to real normalcy! Back to mainstream living! became my motto.

And so I took a vacation from the stationary Movement and its seemingly hellish frustrations. Articles for *The Remnant* lapsed into silence. My trips back to Europe turned away from contacts with exotic traditionalist cells and towards the Riviera for basic, healthy, physical exercise. I took to dancing rather than lecturing, preparing meals from scratch with fresh ingredients rather than polishing notes lambasting Cardinal Gibbons and Bishop Ireland. In my hunger for normalcy and longing for a return to the mainstream of life, I even did something I never would have thought possible just a short time before–I abandoned my Eastern Catholic churches and became a lector for the *Novus Ordo* at my local Greenwich Village parish, Our Lady of Pompeii.

Not that I cut off all my ties with the Movement in those years of backsliding. My companions were still almost exclusively Traditionalists, thus giving my escapade the telltale tinge of a day of hooky from a school which would inevitably call me back to its classrooms. Moreover, aside from Dr. Marra, whose summons to lecture for the Roman Forum I could never turn down, another force entered onto the scene to help to keep me honest during this winter of my discontent. This was the SSPX, in the person of the then Fr. Richard Williamson at the Society's seminary in Ridgefield, Connecticut.

It is true that I am one of those people who has often been quite stunned by some of the things that the now Bishop Williamson has said regarding the Church and the world situation. Nevertheless, his intellectual curiosity, his pastoral solicitude for my soul, and his personal friendship pulled me back from playing with a pointless existence that could easily have slid into the despair that once wore me down so miserably in Oxford. He actually did want to hear what I said about Americanism and Pluralism, and invited me to talk to his seminarians about its dangers…more than once, and in pleasant settings to boot! Further still, he wanted me to lecture not only on contemporary evils, but on my own field of expertise, on Church History in general, as well. This forced me back to the sources of the Tradition for another and still more comprehensive "refresher course."

Once this refresher course began, I quickly had to admit that even if the Movement were all too stationary, the mainstream was hurtling yet farther into Outer Space on its journey to nowhere. Really, no matter how much I had wanted to be "part of something," and recognized that Traditionalists were suffering due to their isolation, I never could flee from the fact that the world at large was nothing other than acceptable society's Twilight Zone. Grateful as I was to the fine pastor of my parish church, which was infinitely saner than most around me, it just could not become my permanent spiritual home. Attendance at family funerals in that ecclesiastical wilderness west of the Hudson, outside relatively conservative New York, showed that liturgies were degenerating at an ever-greater pace. The presence of pianos in the sanctuary had begun to give what ought to have been a somber setting the flavor of a tacky cocktail lounge. Each time I spoke with rarely seen relatives and old acquaintances at these events, whole new chunks of doctrine, morality, and history seemed to have disappeared from their collective memories.

All this meant that when *Ecclesia Dei Adflicta* was finally published, and St. Agnes Church in New York City decided to take advantage of it to restore the Traditional Mass to its Sunday liturgy, I needed only one week to "jump ship" and exchange my lectern for a *St. Andrew's Daily Missal*. Within a fortnight I had donned an acolyte's cassock. A short time after that, I was writing for *The Remnant* again, renewing my contacts with Michael Davies, accepting lecture invitations, and, eventually, working—till they, alas, tired of me—with Una Voce America.

This does not mean that the situation in the Traditionalist world had perceptibly improved in the years of my vacation, from 1985-1988. In some respects, the same partial explanations for the collapse of Christendom were being proclaimed, rehashed, and commented upon even more loudly, insistently, and pedantically than before, with the dangers of the Blog still lurking, unimagined, in the technological underbrush.

Catholic Traditionalism now made its fourth self-validating appearance in my life. This time it appeared to give me advice regarding how to deal with the problems of Catholic Traditionalism itself! My recent "refresher course" in the fullness of the Tradition, urged upon me by the head of a Society seminary, had given me the final push to listen once more to what it was that the Tradition had to teach. Traditionalism again reminded me that one had to "dive in" and use all the natural and supernatural tools available to a man if he were to defeat dangerous influences of all sorts. Dealing with the "problem" of Traditionalists was nothing other than a variant of dealing with the problem troubling me at Oxford. My fellow Traditionalists had to be exposed to more than a lecture, more than an intellectual argument, in order to be won over to an understanding of the evils of an Americanist and Pluralist world. They needed to have the totality of Catholic Faith and culture placed before their minds, souls, and bodies to make the point that my mere words could not describe. My duty was to find a way to create a holistic environment in which they could live, for a time, in a microcosm of a truly Catholic order, and then, by confronting what they experienced with their ordinary daily reality, come to make the same kinds of judgments respecting the deleterious effects of Americanism, Pluralism, and the Anglo-Saxon Enlightenment on Christendom that I had made.

Dr. Marra gave me the means to move forward with this project when he decided, in 1991, to put me in charge of the Roman Forum. This allowed me to gather the funds to create an annual "Catholic Commune" which, like the Chartres Pilgrimage, which I discovered about the same moment, shaped a "time out of time" leaving an indelible imprint on those who participated in it. I had tried something similar, on a much smaller scale, in Venice, in 1985, just before I threw my hands up and went on vacation from the Movement, leaving the project stillborn. This time, the concept was to come together in a more lasting and fruitful form.

Once again, a chance (or providential) visit to the Institute of Christ the King at Gricigliano in Tuscany, introduced me to Cardinal Alfons Stickler and the beauty of the Solemn Pontifical Mass of the Traditional Rite. Cardinal Stickler, with the encouragement and aid of Mgr. Gilles Wach, accepted the Roman Forum's invitation to come to St. Agnes in February of 1992 to inaugurate the work of our "Catholic Commune"–an Institute inspired by Dietrich von Hildebrand's "Incarnation-drunk" vision. This Institute, meeting annually at Gardone Riviera, on Lake Garda in northern Italy, would allow Traditionalists a chance to live a "time out of time" where Catholic principles reigned supreme; where they could eat, drink, sing, play, study, and worship, as Traditional Catholics, with all that their heritage had to offer them placed at the center of their existence. In New York, I had only myself to count on to lecture and appeal to the intellect; in Gardone, I had all of nature and supernature as my senior partners. If nothing else would break through a parochial spirit, I was certain that this could do so. If exposure to the light could have an impact on a spirit as weak and wobbly as mine, surely it could have the same impact more speedily and firmly on others made of stronger stuff.

In the summer of 1982, I found myself in Paris with an unexpected sum of money at my disposal. I decided I wanted to live a week enjoying everything that the *Ville lumière* could legitimately offer me. Up to that point, I had been traveling on the cheap and was in a desperate state of personal disrepair. Once I bought a pair of shoes without holes in them, I realized how ridiculous my worn out trousers appeared. When this problem was remedied, my wretched shirt clearly stood out in all its misery and had to be replaced. That done, I quickly perceived how badly I needed a decent haircut. Everything bodily in order, I marched off to my first museum and immediately recognized that I was terribly, terribly lonely. In short, my decision to enjoy Paris properly caused me to see that much more work was required of me than I at first had bargained for.

When I hopped on the train from Hoboken in 1970 I first got off at the stop marked Catholic Traditionalism. Here I met serious men of joyful spirit; men who understood that all of us make mistakes and backslide in our efforts to do the Good and take possession of the Beautiful; men who emanated a truly noble sense of humor about their own limitations as they played their part in the Drama of Truth.

What my Incarnation-drunk Catholic Traditionalists taught me when I arrived at their destination was that Tradition and Traditionalism were not an end in themselves. They were valuable precisely because they were always a way station; a way station to Christ, to Christ's Mystical Body, and to an understanding of just how much every aspect of grace and nature must be nurtured and loved as a means of leading us to the light of the Beatific Vision. In other words, embracing Tradition was like embracing Paris and coming swiftly to the realization that one's work had just begun when the initial decision was taken. The trip begun in Hoboken had to continue ever onward and ever upward. To turn my back on Tradition would be to abandon a journey to the Father of Lights and eternal joy. To turn my back on Tradition would end with the abandonment of eternal joy, life in an arrogant, unenlightened, and ultimately *unnatural* nature left to its own self-limiting devices, and an eternity in a self-created hell.

Dr. John Rao is an Associate Professor of History at St. John's University in New York City; D.Phil. from Oxford University (UK); author of *Americanism and the Collapse of the Church in the United States* and *Removing the Blindfold*. He is the former president of Una Voce America, and is Chairman of the Roman Forum, which holds its Summer Symposium every summer at Lake Garda in Italy.

Edwin Faust

Lost and Found

I arrived on the train from Saarbrucken late in the evening. I had been traveling the better part of twenty-four hours, and although possessed of the near physical indefatigability of youth, a certain weariness of spirit weighed on me. The journey had not only been long but anxious: a blind leap into the abyss.

I had a few weeks previously severed all ties to my former life: dropped out of graduate school, broken my engagement, sold my car, given away most of my possessions and bought a plane ticket to Europe, having no notion of what I would do when I arrived. Like a character in a Tennessee Williams play, I was trying to recapture in space what I had lost in time. I imagined, or rather hoped, that in casting myself into a sea of experiences I would somehow be borne to a new shore where my life's meaning would be made plain, my path made clear.

The first results of my experiment had proved disheartening. I sat in a rail car listening to people converse in a language I did not understand; I watched the countryside roll by in twilight until the shadows deepened and merged into a black expanse dotted by distant clusters of electric lights that appeared as cold and unwelcoming as the enveloping gloom. At intervals, the train would halt at a platform where over the wall of a red brick station hung a sign announcing the name of a town, a name that meant nothing to me and reinforced my sense of being a stranger in a strange land.

When at last the sign read "Heidelberg," I grabbed my duffle bag and stepped off the train. There was a desk at the station where one could enquire about accommodations. The attendant, a middle-aged woman with sharp, appraising eyes, looked me over and wrote down an address where the proprietress took in short-term boarders; she then pointed me to a taxi stand where I gave the piece of paper to a driver. In a few minutes I found myself knocking on a door in Erwin-Rhode Strasse. The door was at length opened by a large man who asked me brusquely what I wanted. I answered in English that I wanted a room.

"Amerikaner?" he asked in a tired way.

I nodded and he motioned for me to follow him. At the end of a narrow hall he opened a door and, after depositing the requested number of marks in his palm, I found myself sitting on a bed, wondering what to do next. I then realized with surprise that I was hungry, for I had not eaten since leaving New York. Somehow, I had forgotten about food during the brooding hours of my trip. I opened the door and saw my host about to disappear through another door at the opposite end of the hall. I said "Excuse me," in German. He turned with a look of annoyance and asked that I speak to him in English.

"I'm rather hungry," I said.

He gave me directions to a place where I could get food and drink and told me the door to the house was never locked but to be quiet when I returned. I thanked him, he said nothing, and I ventured into the night air.

As I walked along the narrow streets, fear gave way to fascination. Never had I been so far away from home or in a place so different from all I had known. The town was decidedly pretty and the sandstone castle on the hill, illuminated by spotlights, appeared to watch over the valley like a benevolent monarch of immemorial title. A sense of Providence reawakened in me and I was buoyed by the feeling that all would be well.

The windows of the gasthaus to which I had been directed glowed with golden light. It seemed a welcoming place, and no sooner had I taken a table and ordered a glass of wine than I was approached by the member of a group that sat nearby: two men and three women. The man who spoke to me was an RAF warrant officer, stationed near Frankfurt, and his companion was a U.S. soldier: both were on leave and had attached themselves to the three young ladies, American girls touring the country. I was asked to join them, thus evening out the equation, and did so gladly. We were a lively party and the RAF officer, Stan, knew where drinks were to be had in most every quarter of the town, which we canvassed extensively.

The first streaks of dawn were appearing faintly in the sky above the hills when I returned to my room—ever so quietly, if a bit unsteadily—and slipped beneath a down comforter and into a deep sleep. I awoke in mid morning to the sight of a woman standing in the open doorway and staring down at me. She had dark hair and large dark eyes. Her mouth was full and sensual and a cigarette hung loosely from her pursed lips. She was not young, but not quite middle aged, and although her looks were no longer fresh, she remained handsome. I sat up in bed and said hello. She did not answer. After a long pause she said, "Why are you here?"

I became conscious of the inappropriateness of the situation and asked her who she was.

"I am Elizabeth. This is my house. Why are you in it?"

There was something beyond bold curiosity in her manner; something threatening. I had the sense that I was being tested and that were I to give the wrong answer, I would be invited to leave her house.

"To see the world and have a good time," I said with strained nonchalance.

She sniffed disapprovingly.

"Why are you here?" she repeated with a note of impatience.

"Because I'm lost," I said, and in so saying surprised myself but realized that I had spoken truly and had pleased Elizabeth.

"You can stay here for awhile," she said. "I'll tell you when to leave."

The interview thus came to an end and I sat there marveling about the circumstance into which I had fallen, or perhaps, been led.

In the days that followed, I explored the town, drank immoderately, kept late hours and had many curious conversations with my landlady. She was, I discovered, a notorious local character and the authoress of stories and poems that were published in avant-garde periodicals and well received by the more radical elements in the arts and academic communities. The large, surly man who had admitted me on my first night was her live-in companion, Johan, who had come to her door ten years earlier to interview her for a paper he was doing as a student at the university. He never went back to the university and filled his days acting as lover, house boy and intellectual foil for Elizabeth, whose moods were varied but whose tone was uniformly imperious.

She told me I was rather stupid, as were most Americans, but that I was "better material" than were most Europeans. What she liked about me and my countrymen, I took it, was our naiveté and openness. We were suitable for molding and she liked to play the part of sculptress. Her own race were more obdurate and smug, she said. My second day at her house I awoke to find a book laid by my bed: an English translation of a collection of aphorisms by Nietzsche, whom I knew Elizabeth much admired but who was little more than a name to me.

I was allowed the privilege, not extended to other boarders, of having morning coffee in Elizabeth and Johan's kitchen, after which I would take my book and proceed to a rather famous hillside path called the Philosophers' Walk. At a certain bend in the path was an outcropping of rock, a level platform suitable for sitting on cross-legged and surveying the town and surrounding countryside. It became my habit to make my way to this place of meditation and there to remain for a few hours, alternately reading passages of Nietzsche and staring at the waters of the Neckar River, where a ray of sun illumined its own path, one that shone like a ripple of diamonds on a strip of black velvet: a cosmic Philosophers' Walk that promised enlightenment of a rich and unearthly sort.

I found Nietzsche often obscure, occasionally lucid, but never dull. After two weeks I had arrived at certain ideas that I attributed, rightly or wrongly, to Nietzsche's inspiration: I took as the new guide of my life the notion of eternal recurrence. I don't know that I understood it then, nor even now, but it meant to me that one should live each day—if possible, each moment—in such a way that one would gladly repeat the experience. The test of whether one were living well and wisely rested precisely in this: Would one be eager to do the same thing again? It seemed that to live in such a way would require a keen sense of awareness that rose above all that was routine and banal. Most people were sleep-walking, I believed, and I was determined to be as fully awake as my powers permitted.

I adopted Elizabeth's way of shunning small talk and social conventions and relied upon my intuition about people to say to them only that which seemed worth saying. Often, I remained silent, appraising those about me, waiting to see if I were inspired to speak. I tried to see everything—people, nature, myself—with the utmost clarity. Within a few weeks, I felt ready to leave Heidelberg, to break the spell of Elizabeth and become my own master. She approved.

I stayed for the fall wine festival, an event that passed the test of eternal recurrence, then headed south, hitchhiking to warmer climes as the winter approached. But as the weeks rolled by and the months piled up, I found that aspiring to be the superman puts a strain on one's nerves. I found myself at times running away from the clarity I had so earnestly sought; taking refuge in the pleasant fog of intoxication; enjoying the exchange of pleasantries. I began to realize that many of the social conventions I had held in disdain have a subtext: that what appear to be mundane and meaningless conversations are often weighted with complicated thought and emotion, obliquely communicated; that this art of indirection helps us to express the otherwise inexpressible; to say in code that which is too delicate to be phrased in the clumsiness of blunt speech. I began to see Elizabeth's shunning of conventional talk as somewhat juvenile and boorish: an unmannerly way of showing off and trying to gain the advantage of someone through shocking them. And I wondered whether Nietzsche's ideas could be sanely applied in real life. I also entertained the possibility, with some relief, that I was not fitted to be the superman.

But what was I fitted to be?

When Elizabeth had asked me why I had come to Europe and I had answered "Because I'm lost," I had spoken honestly. When I entered high school in 1963, life had a single purpose: salvation. And salvation was only to be found in the Catholic Church. By the time I graduated in 1967, all of that had changed. The Second Vatican Council had intervened. Whether the council merely exposed the fragility of the Catholic edifice or undermined its solid structure is arguable. It seems that the faith must have played a somewhat superficial role in our lives for its institutional expressions to have been swept away so quickly and easily and on such thin pretexts.

By the time I graduated college in 1971, the church had plunged precipitously into its post-Vatican II madness and society, as a consequence, had also lost its sanity. Madness reigned. And in this madness I was expected to find a place for myself; to chart a career, start a family, buy a home, build equity, diversify a portfolio, climb the ladder of success, plan for retirement–in short, to behave in the prescribed ways as though it all still made sense. But it made no sense. How could a sane man acclimate himself to a lunatic asylum? How could you set out to live life when life appeared to have no purpose? It was a game without rules; a play without a plot. It seemed to me and to many of my contemporaries that we were cut off from the past; that if we were to give meaning to our lives, we must do so with little help from the usual quarters: our elders and their traditions.

Going to a strange country was in its way an escape from my native land, which had also become a strange country. No matter where I turned, I felt alienated, but it is somehow more bearable to feel this way in a foreign place than in one's own home. Travel also allowed me to postpone making any serious decisions about my future. I knew that my money would not last long, but for however long it did last, I would be given a reprieve from a responsibility I dreaded.

When I said I was lost, I meant that I had lost a unified vision of life, and it was this I wanted so desperately to recover. And so

I looked for it in many places: in the writings of Nietzsche and in many other books. I tried on idea after idea, like so many changes of clothes, to see which one suited me best. And when I grew tired of thinking, I found respite in the riot of the senses. But after a while, patterns form, and license becomes habit. Even dissipation can fall into a routine. And then one longs to escape those very things that once were an escape. But where is there to go?

After a year of wandering about Europe, collecting experiences, I was still lost; so I came home, or to what remained of my home, and I tried various jobs, none of which lasted; and I lived in various places, never for very long. I was still postponing my life, waiting for some event or idea or person that would lend it meaning and direction. I lived on the East Coast and the West Coast and parts in between; in mountains, by the seashore, in the cities, in the country; I tried sensuality and asceticism; gravity and frivolity; society and solitude. But always I ended in the same state of confusion and near despair. And I was getting older. The world forgives the young their rootlessness and lack of serious purpose, but there comes a time when forgiveness ends and the no longer young wanderer is regarded simply as a bum. I had become a bum.

My thirtieth birthday found me residing in a small rented house in a barrio in Santa Fe, New Mexico, working as a window washer. When we are young, we seldom give thought to all that it means to grow old. We can no more imagine our aging that we can imagine our death. But at the age of thirty the thought was powerfully borne in on me: I would live to be old. I also knew that I did not wish to be an old window washer. I felt immensely tired of everything, most especially myself; yet, I couldn't rouse enough energy or enthusiasm to change my situation. I had reached rock bottom. I was nobody going nowhere.

I celebrated my birthday by walking aimlessly around town, lashing myself with such thoughts. For no particular reason, I wandered into a book store and began listlessly surveying the rack that offered self-help through psychology, diet, exercise, astrology, crystals, aura-balancing and religion. One volume caught my attention. Its cover bore the face of a man, a Hindu, and I felt an intuitive connection with him. I lifted the book from the rack and began to peruse its pages. I had long ago run through all the New Age remedies to life's ills and found them wanting, but for some reason, I bought the book and carried it home, and on my way I became aware of some faint resurgence of my flattened hope.

The book was a spiritual autobiography, a Hindu counterpart to Augustine's *Confessions*. Much of the material was familiar to me, as I had studied Vedanta and various forms of yoga, but a mysterious thrill seized me whenever I opened its pages. The master, let's call him Baba, claimed that one could not become free, *moksha*, without receiving the grace of an enlightened being, a genuine guru. The book, though punctuated by paeans of praise to his teacher, was chiefly concerned with presenting detailed descriptions of the author's own experiences in meditation: experiences that he assured his readers were available to anyone fortunate enough to seek and receive the guru's grace. Without such grace, he claimed, no amount of learning or ascetic practices could bring one onto the path that would lead to liberation from Maya, that is, from all the pain and delusion of this passing world.

His message was certainly not unique, but his effect on me undoubtedly was. Why? Perhaps it was a measure of my desperation that I felt so attracted to him; perhaps it was something more, something preternatural, as I later came to believe. I formed a desire to see this man and, as though on cue, I learned that a local group of his devotees ran a weekly meditation session in a home not many blocks from where I lived. I went there and discovered that he would soon leave India for another tour of North America. He had already established his U.S. headquarters at a sprawling complex in the Catskill Mountains. I was tempted to make the pilgrimage, but hung back, remembering so many of my failed adventures and fearing that this might prove to be just one more.

One of the devotees had given me a picture of Baba, which I hung in my bedroom and which came to have an increasingly hypnotic effect on me. I would find myself staring at his face for long periods, unaware until later of how much time had elapsed;

and during these trances my thoughts would fall away, the clamor in my brain grow fainter, more distant, until it was replaced by a quiet and gentle euphoria. When my thoughts did return, they appeared to be less important, less my own, too, as though I were faintly conscious of some senseless jabbering by an intruder. Then, one night, I had a dream unlike any other I could recall. I dreamt I was sitting in the house where I had grown up, watching the staircase, waiting for something; then, I saw descending the staircase a figure in a long orange robe, such as that worn by Hindu monks. I did not see his face, for as he approached I fell to the ground, prostrated myself, reached my fingers toward his feet, then felt his hand on my back, making some sort of adjustment to my spine. At that instant, I awoke and sensed heat rising in my spine from its base toward my neck. I had the unshakable feeling that something significant had happened to me.

At the next meeting of the meditation group, I told a few of the devotees about my dream. They nodded knowingly. "You've been given *shaktipat*," one said. This is the Sanskrit word for the guru's grace. "It's a powerful form of initiation, to receive it in a dream," the leader of the group said. "You'd better go see Baba."

And so I did.

I had little money, so I hitchhiked from Santa Fe to New York and spent my last few hundred dollars to pay for my stay at the ashram and to attend a program called "The Intensive." The Intensive consists of mantra chanting, talks by devotees, talks by Baba, translated from Hindi by an interpreter, and the chief thing, a meditation session during which the lights are lowered and Baba passes through the sitting crowd, touching people's heads with his wand of peacock feathers or pressing his thumb against their foreheads. The heavy smell of musk perfume marks his approach and a variety of noises follows in his wake: crying, laughter, strange words, animal sounds; feelings of intense joy, overpowering sorrow, visions of lights. Some people simply pass out, their heads lowered to the floor, where they remain until the end of the session. These reactions are called *kriyas* and are supposed to have a purgative effect on consciousness, freeing the subject from all that binds him to this world: karma from lives past and present. The purpose of the guru is to initiate these *kriyas*. When the devotee is completely cleansed of karma, he, too, becomes realized, enlightened, a free soul, one with God. Such is the belief. But this liberation may require a lifetime of meditation; perhaps, several lifetimes. Above all, it requires *shaktipat*, the guru's grace.

My stay at the ashram brought me many vivid experiences in meditation. I was told by veteran devotees that I had been especially blessed. After a few weeks, I left, convinced that, at long last, I had found the real thing. Nothing seemed to matter now. If the world regarded me as a bum or a fool, so much the worse for the world. I had found truth. I was blessed. All that I need do is allow the *shakti* to work. All else was insignificant. I returned home, broke, and spent the winter chopping and selling wood. The next few years found me working a variety of jobs, getting away on occasion for short stays at the ashram in the Catskills until, one summer, I was invited to join the staff as a night security guard. I accepted.

Now, I was free to dedicate myself totally to my spiritual practices. The ashram was quiet and largely empty most of the year. It only came alive for a month or two during the summer when the guru was in residence. So I led a pleasant monastic life in the mountains, patrolling the grounds at night, seeing that all was safe, and spending my days alone in my room, sleeping, meditating, reading. I received a small stipend and my meals were cooked for me in the dining hall, so I rarely had reason to venture beyond the front gates. And I would be less than honest if I did not admit that the two insular years I spent at the ashram were among the happiest in my life. Never had I known such peace. I rested in my faith as in a high and remote hermitage far removed from all the troubles of the world. I was still growing older, but old age now meant drawing nearer to the ultimate beatitude. Time had become my friend.

I was now and again assailed by doubts: could it be that the truth was known only by a few thousand devotees of a Hindu holy man? Did it not seem improbable? Yet, there were precedents, as with the apostles. And why had God created a world of illusion in the first place? The answer was that the world was the Divine *Lila,* or play. It was a form of amusement for the deity. The answer seemed superficial and unsatisfying. And what about evil? Well, that was just karma. But what was karma? How did it originate? The reasoning appeared to be circular. We were told, of course, that the mind was the enemy; that were we to give it free rein, it would lead us into endless torments and delusions. Trust the guru. Trust the *shakti.*

Ah, yes, the *shakti.* And the *kriyas.* It was the reality of these experiences in meditation that answered all questions. Experience, after all, simply and undeniably exists; it is beyond thought. Or is it?

It was during the quiet of the winter months that these questionings became most persistent, yet, an hour's meditation and they were banished—for a time. One night, as the snow fell gently on the surrounding hills and I made my rounds of the grounds and the buildings, I noticed a light burning in the ashram library. Someone had been careless, I thought, and went there to turn off the light and lock the door. But I paused inside the room and surveyed the rows of books. It wasn't much of a library: only two bookcases and a few chairs in a small room. The books were about mysticism: Hindu, Sufi, Buddhist and Christian. I had not frequented the library, for I had a large collection of my own books, but I thought I might take a volume with me to help pass the hours until dawn. My eyes fastened on a title: *Ascent of Mount Carmel,* by St. John of the Cross. I had tried to read it many years before and had found it exceedingly strange and almost unintelligible. But I took it with me and perused it as I sat at my security desk by the front entrance, waiting for my relief.

As I read, I felt the sort of thrill that had seized me seven years earlier when I had first read Baba's book. I had the sense that Providence had placed this book in my hands for a purpose I could not yet discern. When I returned to my room, I read until my eyes grew tired and sleep overcame me; when I awoke, I immediately picked up the book and resumed where I had left off.

Love in the Ruins

The early chapters seemed to confirm me in my path, as they dealt with the necessity to detach oneself from the pleasures of the senses. All their advice and admonitions accorded with my ascetic practices. It was when St. John began to treat of experiences in meditation and contemplation that I realized he was counseling me to reject all that I had accepted as the guarantee of the authenticity of the guru and his teachings. He even named specific experiences highly prized by devotees, such as the visions of lights, the waves of bliss, inner sounds and apparitions. All of these, the saint warned, are rooted in the senses, internal or external, and in the imagination. They may come from God, or the demons, or be the product of our own invention. His standing order is to reject them. Totally. One is neither to become attached to them in memory, reason about them nor desire them. To do so is to open oneself to delusions, human or demonic. Even if the experiences come from God, he warns, we may misunderstand their meaning and allow them to become a source of vanity. We will lose nothing by turning away from them, he assures us, for God will do His work in our souls as He pleases, and He prizes our good intentions above our curiosity and longing for the exotic.

I found St. John's reasoning simultaneously comforting and troubling. It freed me from my thralldom to the admittedly fascinating occurrences in meditation, but it also stripped me of my certainty that I had found the true path to God. I could not doubt that St. John was right, yet, he cast me into a spiritual no-man's land. What was I to do now?

Reading the *Ascent*, however, had another effect on me: it roused memories of my boyhood devotion. I began to re-examine the claims of the Catholic faith, casting aside all the stupidities of the post-conciliar debacle and concentrating on essential doctrine. I bought a copy of the New Testament and spent most of my spare time reading and pondering passages from the Gospels, particularly that of St. John. I felt increasingly uncomfortable in the ashram and studiously limited my contacts with other devotees. I avoided the dining hall and subsisted mostly on a cache of fruit, rice cakes and bottled water.

One afternoon, shortly after waking, I felt a strong desire to take a long walk, to get away from the ashram. It was winter, but I decided to brave the cold and stuffed a few provisions into my pockets along with the New Testament. I made my way to a dense wood beyond the bounds of the ashram property. A rough path led into the forest for about a hundred yards, then ended; I proceeded into the trackless wilderness until the ground began to climb and rocks and boulders appeared. I came to a clearing amid a grove of oak trees where I found an outcropping of rock like a flat table jutting from the hillside. I climbed onto it and sat there cross-legged and began to read St. John's Gospel.

Thus, I formed a daily routine. I spoke very little to anyone, and my job afforded me the solitude I desired. One afternoon, after assuming my accustomed perch atop my rock table, I read the passage in which St. Peter denies Our Lord. A terrible sadness overwhelmed me: I felt sorry for Peter and thought of how, later, he would have given anything if only he could take back those words of betrayal. I felt a kinship with Peter, and then a realization of my own betrayal swept over me. I wept, as Peter must have wept. But I knew, as Peter must have known, that I was forgiven.

When I returned to the ashram, I knew that I was finished with it. I resigned my post and, once again, headed out into the world with no prospects, having only a few dollars, a half-formed faith, but a great hope. I tried to return to the Church; went to confession for the first time in nearly two decades, talked to priests and read voraciously, but I was ill at ease. Something was fraudulent, either in my conversion or in the new teachings I was receiving. Eventually, I came to realize that the faith had been altered by those charged with its protection and propagation. The new Mass became a torment to me, as did many of the homilies I suffered through, but I tried to make the best of it. There seemed no other place left to go.

I had, meanwhile, gotten a job on the copy desk of a daily newspaper, the resort of many ne'er-do-wells. When it was learned that I had an interest in religion, a rare thing in a newsroom, I was asked to contribute a weekly feature on the subject. The paper

Love in the Ruins

published a page every Saturday with announcements of church services and an article on some personality or event of an ecclesiastical nature. While casting about for my weekly topic in the summer of 1988, I came upon a story about a French archbishop who had been excommunicated for disobeying the pope. In my researches, I learned of outposts manned by the Society of St. Pius X and by independent priests where the Traditional Latin Mass was said and the full Catholic faith preached and practiced.

I wrote my article, a rather transparent apologia for Archbishop Lefebvre, but as it was only a religious matter, the agnostic editors either didn't mind or didn't notice its tendentious nature and allowed it to be published. I also traveled that Sunday to the nearest Tridentine Mass at an independent chapel about eighty miles distant.

After Mass, I remained in the chapel to make my thanksgiving and I remembered something ironic the guru had once said: that it doesn't matter if the teacher is false, so long as the disciple is true, for the true disciple sooner or later finds the true teacher.

I had been lost for so many years, had traveled down so many dead-end streets and lived through so many desperate hours, but God had never let me go, for no matter how far astray I went, I carried in my heart a longing for the truth, a desire to know God. And as St. Augustine wrote: "He who seeks God has found Him."

And so, on the verge of middle age, with my unified vision restored, I felt ready to begin life in earnest. I married, had three children in quick order and resigned myself to my job in the newsroom, which I regarded with a measure of gratitude for enabling me to support my family and granting me a modicum of respectability. It was, in other ways, purgatorial: slogging my way through all the dull and poorly written copy I regarded as a way of expiating my sin of sloth. God had given me a small talent for writing and I had never developed it, partly because I was confused but largely because I was lazy. And so I was now reduced to the school-marmish task of correcting the grammar and punctuation and syntax of the marginally literate.

But God is merciful, and St. Paul wrote truly that all things work together for good for those who love God. I continued to read about and ponder the condition of the Church and came to know some well-informed traditional Catholics. One of them suggested that, as I was in the newspaper business, I should write articles for Traditional Catholic publications. I had never considered doing so, but the idea grew on me and, at long last, I submitted a piece. It was published and became the first of more than a hundred such offerings during the past fifteen years.

I know little of theology or philosophy, so I write about what I do know: my life. For I realize that I am but one of many children in this sorry epoch who has felt abandoned by Mother Church and has wandered through strange lands, physically and spiritually, trying to find her again. I tell my stories and try to find in each anecdote something instructive, a bit of good counsel that might be of use to others.

And in doing so I have discovered that nothing goes to waste in the economy of salvation; that every idea, whether it come from Nietzsche or Baba, contains some truth, or else it would have no substance and be inexpressible. I am, in a way, still guided by the notion of eternal recurrence as I now realize that all we do in time gives shape to our eternity; that all of my actions indeed have an everlasting character; that I will forever taste their sweetness or bitterness in heaven or in hell.

And all of my hours of mediation in the ashram taught me how to sit quietly. It is sad how few of us know how to do this, for it is a prerequisite for contemplation, which is the goal of the spiritual life and the vocation of every Catholic. Heaven, after all, will be simply unbroken contemplation. Our Lord told us that eternal life is to know God and Jesus Christ whom He has sent, and we cannot know God if we are constantly bustling about, full of our own thoughts and plans and desires. We have to empty ourselves of all this and make room for God. So the Desert Fathers and the great Carmelite mystics tell us. And so the lure of false mysticism rests on a solid truth: that our true nature can only be realized when we surrender our will in silence to our Creator.

And I learned something else from my years of attachment to Baba: how to be a disciple. This sense of closeness to the master is what so moved the apostles and the early Christians, and is so lacking among many modern Catholics, even those loyal to Tradition. We may disdain the sentimentality of certain Protestants who talk volubly about their "personal relationship with Jesus Christ," mostly because Protestants don't really know Christ or His Church. But a personal relationship with Our Lord is the only way to salvation: "I am the way, the truth and the life. No one comes to the Father except by me."

And I also now realize that one must be patient with those who lack faith, ever hoping for their reclamation and refraining from judgment. For many years I remained away from the Church and the sacraments. I gave ample reason for those who loved me to despair of me, and little promise that I would ever right myself and do anything in the least worthwhile. But God waits for us, sometimes through the greater part of a lifetime, and we never know who He has marked out for His saving grace. Nor can we be certain of our own perseverance. It is part of the mystery of Providence that God sometimes allows us to fall and to wander far away, only to bring us back to Him, wiser through our fall than we were in our former virtue. We learn mercy by receiving mercy.

I am still sometimes assailed by doubts, but these concern the efficacy of my meager scribblings. I wonder whether I am not simply yielding to vanity, imagining that I am capable of saying something significant in however limited a way. But then I remember the story of the talents. Whatever we have, we have from God, be it little or great, and He intends for us to use it well. And who is to say what is little or great? Each of us, I believe, has his part to play in the design of Providence, and if in the course of a long and tortuous life we are at some single moment able to help another on his way to God, we will have done a great thing. *Ad majorem Dei gloriam.*

Edwin Faust has worked as a newspaper journalist for the last twenty-two years. He also writes for *Catholic Family News* and *Latin Mass Magazine* and was, some time ago, a columnist for *The Remnant* and a regular contributor to *The Angelus* magazine. Ed and Kathleen, his wife of twenty-one years, have three children and live in Northfield, New Jersey.

T. Renee Kozinski

Veronica

Traveling along the coast of California on Route 1 between Santa Cruz and Monterey my attention was drawn suddenly from the ethereal beauty of the gilded light falling on sand dunes and Monterey pines with their fingers reaching out to the ocean, to the side of the truck in the next lane. The whole side of the ten-or-twelve-or-sixteen-wheeler was plastered with a photograph of a father frolicking in a pool with two small children clinging to his shoulders. How many processes had this photo gone through, I thought? Were the people even related to one another or were they simply chosen for their photogenic smiles and architectural features? Was there even a pool or was it spliced in later? How much doctoring and coloring and tweaking was done to achieve the desired effect? The juxtaposition between the stunning natural panorama before me and the adulterated image selling pool supplies made my stomach tighten. I felt angry at the use of a poignant, sacred reality–a moment of intimate, familial joy–to sell products. Most things in life are simply too sublime for the mercenary world of commercialism.

I am a convert to Catholicism from Protestantism and I have an artist's soul. Images have been my constant interest and companions from childhood. Within Protestantism, I struggled with the dearth of teaching images; carriers of beauty. I never saw Calvinistic asceticism as stoic pure Christianity, but rather as a fear-based religion with an unbalanced notion of God, a self-righteous iconoclasm paling beside the deep and ancient tradition of image contained in both the Orthodox and Catholic Faiths. Some Protestants do have paintings of Christ, and some are beautiful, but the depth of the *teaching* image, such as the Eastern icon or the liturgies of the ancient Christian churches, is lacking. And the most conspicuous absence is the sublime image in Catholic life: the Mass; the moving image of liturgy, which is the medium by which we understand most fully the truths embodied in the Presence of Christ among us in the Eucharist.

As I went through the process of conversion—which happens before and after entry into the Church—my journey was bound up with image because, as an artist, this is how I understand the deepest things and is what primarily fuels my imagination and most directly teaches my soul. Ever since the bishop crossed my forehead with the chrism oil during my confirmation at St. Agnes' Church in New York City, I have studied and suffered with the present and confusing landscape of the Church in modern times. It has been primarily a dialogue with images and about images, for I believe that images are teachers to the erudite and common alike, just as the astounding stained glass of Chartres Cathedral teaches generations about the doctrines of our Faith and the nature of grace, which falls on us like light. I have searched imagery in modern and tradition liturgies, Eastern Catholic rites, and the *Novus Ordo* Mass with Latin and Gregorian chant, and considered what the imagery of each teaches.

When I "came home to Rome," I was expecting a certain level of image—in part because of my experience as a child living in Greece with the Greek Orthodox faith. I was not prepared for the pabulum of "meal" and "people of God" imagery I found in many modernized Catholic churches. I was angry when I came across certain pictures on the front of some missals in Catholic churches. I detested, in a visceral way, the colored drawings which look like they came right out of a primitive tribe with heads sort of twisted around and hands too large for the body in strange, grotesque "praise" positions. What these images have in common with the picture on the side of the truck in California is an unnatural use of images to *sell* something or to promote an ideological purpose which has nothing to do with seeking the truth. For example, the neo-primitive religious art on the front of a missal promotes the idea of returning to the simplicity of the early Christian Church.

But this "return to the primitive" idea is a lie because it is impossible for a living organism to regain an original state, much like it is impossible for me to return to the eight-year-old child I was. The passage of time in the life of the Body of Christ has, in God's providence, produced an inexorable and irreversible development.

Within the Protestant sects, and especially among my Calvinistic Presbyterian ancestors (of which I have a grandfather who was a pastor), this iconoclasm is a powerful ideology; a very tenet of their faith. It is a reaction to what they perceived as complicated, but meaningless, external practices of Catholics. In a brilliant use of mythology, Calvinists created the ideal of the "early Church" for which the Pauline churches and those of the catacombs in Rome were adapted. This idea is manifested in statements like, "We go straight to Christ," and in the words carved into many Calvinist communion tables, "Do this in remembrance of Me." Remembering is simple and unmysterious, in contrast to the pagan and sophisticated barbarism of Catholic transubstantiation.

In my experience as a Protestant, the Calvinist mythology was clearly imaged in ecclesial architecture and the aesthetic configuration of worship space: the bare cross and the bare wall. The architecture is often a severe beauty–in the older churches especially–with spiring ceilings like pine trees on a German hillside, but pine trees in winter. This architecture reaching upwards in an icy purism is supposed to invoke the simplicity and purism of the early Church, free of such excesses as images of the saints. The crucifix, the great witness of Christianity, is replaced by an empty cross, or by no cross at all. Instead, the pulpit takes precedence, beautifully carved and placed close to the center, the communion table fading beside it in obscurity. The *word* of the preacher is the main sacrament; the simplicity and rationality of logos eclipsing the "mess" created by idols and the pious practices surrounding them. In ancient Catholic and Orthodox churches there is a focal image (in a Catholic church, the wall behind the altar; in an Orthodox church, the iconostasis), but in a Protestant church there is only a bare wall. The bareness is no accident; the lack of image is also a teacher, but of heresy; what Belloc might call the extreme and thus unbalanced warping of the truth.

As a Protestant, this distortion of truth had a profound effect on my life. As a visual artist, I was starving: perhaps because I was more acutely aware of the barrenness and sterility that masqueraded as John-the-Baptist asceticism or because of my childhood immersion in the rich beauty of European culture where I fed on architecture, art, and cultivated landscape which nurtured my soul.

My entry into the Catholic Church was twofold: I sensed within her walls an ancient image–the Ancient of Days as a Body on earth; and I came to see that the towering architecture of Western thought was largely built, cultivated, and kept in the portico of that Church. Within the folds of Holy Mother Church, I was steeped again in culture (cult-ure, the best word to describe it): Gregorian chant, philosophy in her right place as handmaid of theology, and, of course, the plenitude of teaching image; of image beautiful in its reflection of truth. One of the concepts most precious to me is the very Catholic idea of non-utilitarianism, which says an image can be beautiful–just beautiful–and this is good. Thus, I was dismayed to find infiltrators within this rich citadel of the City of God, especially in the form of Protestant or primitive images.

Because of some individual Catholics who teach the erroneous mythology of the "bare and simple" faith, living tradition has been thrown out. Eschewing traditional images as idolatry is but one symptom of a larger heresy, but it is much more influential than we realize. In the West we tend to focus on the rational argument of doctrine and history. Being made in the image of God who "saw and declared it was good," our sight–whether it be spiritual or physical–fires our imagination and the imagination is nursemaid to the soul, feeding it with whatever is burning there.

I still found living tradition in enclaves like violets hanging onto life in the crevices of a stone wall. Coming from the Bare Wall religion, I was struck dumb for a time upon entering a beautiful, old Catholic cathedral. I felt as if I'd come into a treasure house, a holy space filled with the presence of a "cloud of witnesses"; statues, paintings, light-filled images of Marian and Christological truths, and the Suffering One upon His cross above the altar. But He was not alone. There were innumerable saints, some holding flowers and some with lambs kneeling below the cross and looking up at Our Lord. Some of the statues were not well made–they even looked a little garish–but the wooden and plaster toes and hands were worn away by the countless handholdings and caresses of the living. I remembered the Greeks and Russians kissing the icons at the entryway to their churches. I understood from my wide-open childhood that this was the same "looking through" to reality, a crutch of sorts for those in the vale of tears still struggling to live in two worlds, still waiting with tears for the consummation of heaven and earth. It was much deeper than the Bare Wall, for it was connected to thousands of years of human religion, time baptized in the Blood of Christ.

Then I saw the Mass; the procession, the cross, the vestments, and finally the priest coming like a king and at the same time, a victim to the execution, flanked by soldiers in black and white robes. He ascended the altar and prayed for himself and for us. As the soldier-altar boys moved back and forth in unison, the priest, like Homer's pole star, symbol of the Unmoved Mover, stayed still and implored. Under the Crucifix we become present to the Reality through our senses, imagination, and soul, by sounds, words, and tone; by Gregorian chant crafted to encourage meditation and prayer, by the silent witness of the represented saints, and most deeply, by the moving image that is the liturgy of the Holy Sacrifice. If this image is crafted well, organically from two thousand years of Christian tradition and under the inspiration of the Holy Spirit, it is the highest teacher and guide into the center of history and life. It is Calvary and the sharing of the Body of Christ which transforms us individual sinners into a single and glorious Body.

The Holy Mass is a living truth that is too deep and sublime for us to understand cognitively, yet our souls drink it in through our imagination. We know that there it is an essential *person* we meet in a neighbor, but as C. S. Lewis says in *The Problem of Pain*, we know our neighbor through the medium of matter. Thus, the liturgy is like the body of the Mass combining the mediums of symbolism (including the spoken and written word), movement, and imagery. One of the primary images in the perennial Mass of the Church is that of the *Alter Christus*, the priest climbing the altar with the servers in his wake, pulled upwards to the Sacrifice. It is Christ ascending Calvary, pulling along the crowd beyond the rail. That image of the priest's hands with the Host raised upwards at the pinnacle of all people and architecture is what everything in the liturgy builds to; it is the climax of the truth of Christ's sacrifice being relived. After the re-presentation of the crucifixion we see Christ, in the image of the priest, turning from the altar and moving downwards toward the kneeling crowd to feed them like a shepherd. This image stays in our soul as a beacon and reminder of our great hope in Him. After countless exposure to these images, we are indoctrinated into the hope of a benevolent and risen Lord who has gone before us into death and will bring us into His life.

My great dismay at the primitive return and meal images was a reaction against the attempt to wipe away the crown and source of Catholic life. As St. Thomas Aquinas teaches, all knowledge begins in the senses. The medium of learning for the sense of sight is the image, and images fuel our imagination. Images in film, paint, poster, statue, and nature enter into us and make their abode in our souls, taking along with them an underlying meaning and purpose. The more expertly an image is tied to the underlying message of the artist (whether he be a classical artist or an advertiser), the more it is a powerful and permanent teacher.

The camera will not steal your soul, but images can. In the case of a powerful, theologically correct icon, our souls are stolen for God and we see through the icon to heavenly truths. The icon image is meant to change us permanently for the good; to draw us to God. It is meant to be a *veronica*, which means *true icon*. On the other hand, with a perverse image like an advertising-hook, our souls risk being stolen for Satan and the consumer-economic machine. Either that, or we grow protective shells to keep out the constant bombardment of inappropriate emotional images and in doing so become desensitized to the teaching of any true image. We are so accustomed to the image as a prostitute for money and propaganda, that we vacate the place for sacred image in our liturgical life.

Perhaps the Calvinists, Muslims, and the Jews of the Old Testament were on to something in their prohibition against making images, which have such power for evil. Thousands of years ago, the Lord forbade His people from making images of Him or of any creature. He was stripping them; purifying their imaginations and their souls. In the ancient world, images of numerous gods were in every household and caravan. Egypt was especially rife with pagan images, so the Lord brought them out of the habit of seeing gods in every image by forbidding image-making altogether. The Temple in Jerusalem had no icons, statues (except for the four Cherubim on the Ark), or tapestries that could be confused with the Lord Himself dwelling in the Holy of Holies, a place as hidden as the Lord who hid His Face. The people were to worship and to reach Him by faith and sacrifice, by action and word. The only images He gave them on the flight from Egypt were the pillar of fire by night and pillar of smoke by day.

Mysteriously, God allowed Moses to use an image of a snake to heal the Israelites of their snake bites (a punishment for disobedience or sin). How do we read this apparent contradiction? The image of the snake on a cross-stick is spoken of in the tradition of the Church as prefiguring Christ on the cross made sin for our sake. I would argue that it was a pre-figurement of the appropriate use of imagery. In forbidding image-making, but using an image to teach, the Lord taught the Israelites about the power of the image to transmit both lies and truth.

Perhaps we can also understand this contradiction in terms of fulfillment. With the Incarnation, God suddenly became an image! He now had a face we could look upon—a physical image of the Divine, a true fulfillment of Moses' desire to see God's face. Perhaps His people had been purged of imagery for long enough that now they could tell others of Him, of heaven and creation, of the glories of God in His saints and angels, by creating images. These images would be the Gospel for the illiterate and for the child; images that could literally inspire and draw us to God. Perhaps He knew that the world would need to know that He really was a man with normal features, even humble ones, with facial hair and a longish nose, and human eyes that looked upon those who would want others to see Him as well.

A reading of John Paul II's encyclical on the proper use of image in art tells us that images can be used to distort reality and teach lies. However, God also made us with the power and desire to imitate His creative nature in works of art that tell of the beauty of His creation. Each image has a theology and a philosophy behind it. The less skillful the tie between the actual image and its underlying theme or purpose, the less important it is. On the other hand, the context in which an image is placed also determines its use for good or evil. For example, if an Andy-Warhol-esque painting of an anonymous, stick-figure woman is placed above the altar at a church, it becomes evil because it is teaching something distorted. It has been put in a place where it does not belong, and so is understood not as a "universal utilitarian symbol," but as a lying commentary on the nature of a woman and her body. If it is placed on the door of an airport restroom it fulfills a mundane but natural purpose and so does not exert improper power or teach a twisted message.

In the image-impoverished churches of today, much like the Calvinistic, iconoclastic temples of Protestantism, the imagery is often skewed, diffused, or downright twisted to imprint upon one's soul the image of a family dinner or garden concert. There is a spurious motivation, erroneous theology, and confused philosophy behind these liturgical symbols which change the emphasis of the Mass from a sacrifice to a meal: disordered–like the advertisement on the truck driving down the California highway.

This new imagery that focuses on the people of God, the community meal, or a return to simplicity is a sort of 'mere Christianity' which aims at the unification of Christians. But it is a re-presentation of the Passover, the institution of the Eucharist, and not a re-presentation of the sacrifice of Calvary. This meal imagery is less disturbing to the modern mind and easier for ecumenical efforts, but in actuality it is closer to the Jewish Passover or Protestant communion service than it is to the traditional Catholic imagery of the Mass as sacrifice. It is a movement towards *aggiornamento.*

In trying to understand the use of the Passover or family meal imagery, I approached this kind of liturgy with openness and charity. I understood that the Passover was the institution of the Eucharist and a holy feast worthy of remembrance and reverence. But it was incomplete, I saw, or Christ would have stopped there. The real Passover occurred on Calvary, amidst Christ's suffering and bloodshed. The Bread of Life comes to us through this climactic moment, not through the Passover meal. Calvary is what fulfills the earlier image of the Passover and allows us, through the Mass, to feed our souls and bodies. It is not only the central moment of history through which we interpret what came before and after it, but also the true center of the life of the Church. The Mass, as an image-teacher, must reflect this truth clearly and definitively.

A great story has a climax or turning point, the moment in the story where the plot turns in a major way allowing for the resolution. J. R. R. Tolkien calls this the "eucatastrophe," the resolution that resounds as "the sudden joyous turn." Calvary is the turning point, the climax of our life, pointing to the resolution, which is the hope of heaven. The problem with teaching the image of Passover to the exclusion of Calvary in the liturgy of the Mass is that it changes the story. If the climactic image is a Passover meal and not Calvary, what then is the resolution? The "story as teacher" becomes incomplete, and thus we find the desperate attempt to remedy this change by the static images of the "Resurrection Christ" and Protestantized praise music. The seemingly benign and more acceptable image of a Passover meal is a misreading of the Christian story; it skips right over the blood and suffering of a single Man-God on His cross. And as images do, these liturgical symbols-in-action have created their own theology, sometimes unbeknownst to their creators, which twist the soul away from the balance of God and neighbor to the skewed focus on *us*, on a pleasant meal with brothers and sisters, a world without the need for the Cross.

My experience with the Catholic Byzantine liturgy—a liturgy which reminds me of deep and clear water, refreshing and profound and elemental—helped me to understand this. The Byzantine image of heaven is an image that is gained *through* the Holy Sacrifice. The message is clear: heaven is reached because of Calvary; indeed, the Consecration takes place within the confines of the iconostasis (the gate to heaven), that is, in a central place. Thus, the Sacrifice is *not* presented as a meal; it is "the source and summit" of the Christian life, *even in heaven*. Another way to see this is to remember that Christ appeared in His risen body with the wounds of His suffering, wounds that are praised in heaven now and always; the Lamb slain and surrounded by His saints described in the Book of Revelation. The Byzantine rite is a different way of presenting the same emphasis on the Sacrifice on Calvary. As Fulton Sheen describes, it brings *us* to Calvary, rather than the other way round.

I have known many priests and lay people who suffer because of false imagery in modern liturgies and who try their best to heal it. I knew a priest who celebrated the *Novus Ordo* as originally promulgated (which is significantly closer in spirit to the Tridentine Mass than its present derivatives) and I experienced many blessed moments in the London Brompton Oratory. But these long-suffering priests are often completely unsupported in their efforts, and even actively persecuted by those who have been effectively indoctrinated into, in some cases, another faith.

As people are exposed to the beautiful images of the ancient liturgies, they are drawn into the incredible drama that is a gateway into an actual, mystical presence at the center point of history: Calvary. This image, as marginalized and heaped with opprobrium as it has been (what else would we expect from the Cross?), *is* the light of the world. But can we still see it? Because of the plethora of images with which we are constantly bombarded, we have perhaps become less aware of the power they still exert in our souls. A conscious effort to renew our understanding of their power is essential if we want to protect ourselves effectively. We can turn off unnecessary worldly images, live a simpler life, and search for the true image-teachers: beautiful and true liturgy, icons, paintings or statues in the proper theology and context which will help our soul's journey towards God.

I believe that every human being has been given an intrinsic ability to recognize beauty; the true image as opposed to the images which are prostitutes for ideologies. It frightens me to see the sheep of Christ slowly inculcated into a culture that is vulgar, primitive, and mundane. When I lived in Russia, the depth and beauty of the ancient Russia was entwined with the images and beauty of the Orthodox faith; but many of the people in Russia had lost the desire for God and couldn't even imagine past the grey reality which was life in Soviet Russia. The lack of imagination, the death of the true image, was a major reason they lost their desire for the truth. It is a diabolical process which happened in Russia through a near-complete Soviet control of image, and can–and is–happening in the West through the barrage of images which are prostitutes for false religion or for the sale of yet another pool.

T. Renee Kozinski is a mother, teacher, writer and painter (in that order). She is a writing tutor for Wyoming Catholic College, where her husband, Dr. Thaddeus J. Kozinski, teaches the Humanities and Trivium. Mrs. Kozinski received her M.A. in the Liberal Arts from St. John's College in Annapolis, and is a convert to Catholicism from eclectic evangelicalism. She has lived in many different countries, including Afghanistan, Greece, Russia, Costa Rica and Canada. Mrs. Kozinski's essays and paintings can be found on her blog: www.catholicelan.blogspot.com.

Michael J. Matt

It's the Mass that Matters!

When asked what sort of person presumes to elevate himself to the rank of *traditional* Catholic, a wise wag once quipped: *Is there any other sort?*

He may have a point! According to the infallible teachings of Holy Mother Church, a Catholic is by definition a *traditionalist* since his religion rests on the twin foundations of Scripture and Tradition. One who is loath to identify himself with Tradition cannot ingenuously call himself Catholic.

If, on the other hand, the qualifier refers to those disenfranchised Catholics who'd voiced serious concern over the new direction their Church began to take in the late 1960's, when novelty began to supplant Tradition in both liturgy and catechism, then by conviction as well as association quite a number of us today would count ourselves in the company of traditional Catholics.

Why? The short answer is easy: God's good grace. The number of Catholics that left the Church in the decades that followed the promulgation of the *Novus Ordo Missae* is staggering. Churches closed, seminaries emptied, vocations dried up, and there was an alarming exodus from religious life and even the priesthood itself—the statistics tell the whole, sad story. But traditionalists remained in the Church and, their ranks now swelling worldwide, have come to represent the future of the Church. I think Pope Benedict's historic motu proprio *Summorum Pontificum* more or less acknowledges this fact. In France, for example, the number of Catholics attending the traditional Latin Mass is beginning to overtake the number attending the so-called New Mass. Without question, traditionalism is the future of France.

Love in the Ruins

So, grace is the short answer. But for a more in-depth explanation most traditionalists point to some baptism of fire or spiritual restlessness along the road of life that ultimately set them down on the path to Tradition. Alas, in my case this would be something of a stretch. There is no road to Damascus experience on my résumé–no voices from heaven nor lightening above. I can't even lay claim to a decent "conversion story"!

Through circumstances well beyond my control, I was born with the condition...well, if not actually born with it then at least raised in it. My contribution to the present discussion could be entitled *Growing Up Traditional Catholic*.

When I was a child the traditionalist movement was teething. The *Novus Ordo Missae* had just forced itself upon the Bride of Christ and liturgical experimentation was spreading like dementia throughout the lifeblood of the Church. Those who resisted what history would call the "regime of novelty" had not yet organized themselves into a full-fledged movement.

By an accident of birth I showed up around that time. And what a time it was! Currents diverted this way and that by the designs of modernists, liberals, and liturgical hippies were churning into a riptide of conflict in the Church. Theological time bombs were exploding all over the place; nuns and priests were throwing off their old habits as well as the habits of old; and the first pope I remember, Paul VI, seemed to be in a permanent quandary over how to reconcile Tradition with *Aggiornamento*–the catastrophic effort to make the Church acceptable to a modern world learning fast how to hate Christ. Even popes couldn't force the Genie unleashed by the Sexual Revolution and the volcanic eruption of the Second Vatican Council back into the bottle.

No part of the world was spared, and one day the lava flow reached the door of the little stone church in my neighborhood. We didn't know it then, of course, but life was about to change forever.

The parish priest who'd baptized my brother and sisters had built the church practically by hand, volunteered at the little fire department, set up a modest credit union for his parishioners, accepted no state aid for his school, always dressed in the Roman collar and priestly black. You know the type—a rock of stability, delightfully rough around the edges, quick with a joke, and ever apt to be in casual conversation with his friends in heaven. Life for him *was* the Faith!

As he was Catholic straight through he was a traditionalist alright, though no one ever thought to call him that. The old traditions that had molded his priestly character were still disappearing into the smoke of civil war. Life for all Catholics would soon become either an endless trail of tears or a road to nowhere that would eventually wind its way out of the Church.

I was still in short pants at the time but remember the battle that raged that summer. The old pastor and the Latin Mass were losing ground to the new trends. Half his parishioners were against him, half didn't care, and a small faction stood with him as his ship sank beneath the waves. Before long, he was swept out to sea, and folks like my own parents who'd stood with him were swimming in the unfamiliar waters of post-conciliarism.

I remember riding my bike through the church parking lot after the war had ended and seeing slabs of the hacked-up high altar serving as parking curbs—marble metaphors of a Church under siege. Like the Sacrifice itself, the altar of God had been shattered.

Soon, freeways became a part of our Sunday morning experience as we (like many other families) joined the ranks of the "Roamin' Catholics"—disillusioned folks who'd move from church to church trying to find something that resembled the Catholic Mass.

Then there were the Sunday morning walk-outs. Ours was a family of nine children, so when my father decided he'd had a stomach full our dash for the exits wasn't subtle. Midway through the sermon (sorry, by then it had become a "homily"), my father would groan from the far end of the pew: "Good Lord, this is heresy!" That's when we knew we'd be finishing Sunday observance with the Rosary in the station wagon. This went on for a time until we finally landed in a Ukrainian Catholic Church and fell in love with the Liturgy of St. John Chrysostom.

Love in the Ruins

All throughout the 1970's and '80's, however, there were the Men in Black–travelling priests from around the world who'd resisted the regime of novelty and had gradually set up an underground railroad for Latin Mass Catholics. My father's house was a regular stop for Fr. Urban Snyder, Fr. Harry Marchosky, Fr. Lawrence Brey, Fr. James Dunphy, Fr. Paul Crane, Fr. Vincent Miceli, Fr. Brian Houghton, Fr. Clarence Ludwig, and a long list of the first traditionalists–the pioneers, if you will. Men who were traditionalist before it was cool to be "Trad."

My earliest recollections of the Latin Mass are set in the basement of my father's house. I remember the murmur of the Latin and the scent of altar linens, candle wax, wine, and communion bread. I can still see the hems of albs and the soles of black shoes as the various priests came and went in and out of my childhood, worshipping God in the old way. There in the catacomb chapel, vestments would swish back and forth before my eyes in the mystical dance of liturgy, as those Men in Black–priests forced out of their sanctuaries and into basements like ours–ascended homemade altars of God.

The Masses were held in secret, of course, prompting children to imagine that the "Queen's men" were to break down the door at any moment. The old Latin Mass was illegal, or so we'd been told; but here and there it was being kept alive by new Edmund Campions–brave priests who'd given up everything from pension to position in the name of preserving the most beautiful thing this side of heaven. At their sides I learned to serve the old Mass; at their feet, I learned to live the old Faith.

To take credit for being a traditional Catholic would be like taking credit for being an American. I was born here, and all the credit belongs to them–the immigrants from the old Church who showed us how to survive in the new one. Homeschooling in hiding, hearing Mass in secret, fearing the advance of communists and modernists alike–this was the reality of those days. But the travelling priests–with the joy of the martyrs in their eyes and the faith of the saints in their hearts–managed to carve that reality into a bona fide Catholic counterrevolution.

Michael J. Matt

I was ten years old when I received the sacrament of Confirmation. In those days traditional Catholic families didn't have a lot of options when it came to receiving the old sacraments. Many traveled great distances to find good priests. Others waited for years rather than subjecting their children to bishops who'd seemingly lost the Faith.

My father saw an opportunity in 1976 to have his children confirmed, even though some of us were underage. He invited a bishop—a friend of his and a man he admired a great deal—to come here to St. Paul for a reception. At the same time, arrangements were made to offer the traditional form of the sacrament of Confirmation.

The setting was the small country church where our old pastor had been put out to pasture. It was one of those churches that no longer exist, I suppose, other than in memory. I can remember being intrigued by the organ, for example, which was operated manually by the feet of the organist while he played the keys with his fingers. They called them pump organs, which gives you an idea of how far back this church went.

The Church of the Annunciation was like a time machine, really, with its groaning, old oil-burning furnace in the winter, its lack of air conditioning in the summer, its wooden floors that creaked beneath the feet of communicants, and those open windows that in the spring let in the good country air, permeated with the scent of grass and ploughed earth and cows. Beyond a stand of towering pines just outside the windows, leaning gravestones marked the final resting places of those fortunate ones who'd lived and died in peace beneath the steeple of the old Church.

My father parked the station wagon on the gravel driveway, and I jumped out into dusty sunshine. It was a big day, and I was nervous as my mother ran a comb through my hair.

Next I remember kneeling at the rail on a green pad, trying to collect my thoughts, remember my catechism, say my prayers, and ready myself for the big moment. I was distracted, of course, as little boys usually are. In a moment a famous French Archbishop would stand before me and usher the Holy Ghost into my soul. How does a child of ten process such a thought!

Then it began—the formula of Confirmation, recited in soft voice and unfamiliar accent. My forehead was anointed with holy chrism, and I lifted my face to receive the much anticipated "slight blow on the cheek," symbolizing the new status as soldier of Christ. For just an instant I was looking into the eyes of Archbishop Marcel Lefebvre. That moment was never to be forgotten. The images of that day long ago are forever seared into my memory—bright sunshine, green fields, a dusty gravel road, a white framed church, my mother and sisters, my father and brother, and an Archbishop, his hand raised in blessing, the same light of the martyr's joy in his eyes.

To my grave it will be my contention that on that day I was in the presence of a saint. May history prove me right!

We were trying to survive in a Church at war. Some men—like Archbishop Lefebvre—remained on the field of battle when nearly everyone else was retreating. They gave their lives in defense of holy Tradition, the touchstone of which was then and is now the immemorial Tridentine Mass.

Yes, I know, they don't call it that anymore. Now it's the "Extraordinary Form" or some such thing. But for me it will always be the Tridentine Mass because that is what *they*—Lefebvre, my father, Davies, von Hildebrand—called it when they stood against the whole modern world in its defense. It was the Roman Rite, offered in the ancient tongue by a priest who faced the altar of God as priests had done for thousands of years. It was the Sacrifice of Mass codified by St. Pius V at a dogmatic Council that forever cast in iron Catholic doctrine and liturgy against the great assault on both that was the Protestant Revolution.

"It's the Mass that matters"! Over and over again, the early traditionalists had reminded the world: "It's the Tridentine Mass that matters!" They knew exactly what it was. They knew that important aspects of it predated Trent by some fifteen hundred years. But by referring to it affectionately as the "Tridentine Mass," they lashed themselves in perpetuity to the mast of Catholic Tradition—

the dogmatic Council of Trent. And in the uncertain waters and tossed seas of the post-conciliar era, they followed a course set by Catholics in sixteenth-century England during the Western Uprising and in France during the holy war for altar and throne in the Vendée. Their fight for the Mass would define them. Their fight for the Faith changed history.

Archbishop Lefebvre would be "excommunicated" for his dogged defense of all things Tridentine. But because of him a worldwide Catholic restoration was born.

My friend and mentor Michael Davies worked himself into an early grave for Tradition, as did the great Hamish Fraser and John Senior.

My father gave up everything except Faith and family in its name. After thirty years in harness as editor of *The Wanderer*, Walter Matt left birthright behind in order to defend Tradition in that same basement where the Latin Mass was preserved in secret—*The Remnant's* nursery. Soon there was one and then two AB Dick 360 printing presses howling away down there at all hours, cranking out newspapers and pamphlets that cried out like the very stones in defense of Tradition.

In 1956, young Hungarians defended their homeland against Soviet tanks with brooms and whatever else they could lay their hands on. They were crushed to death by Communists but immortalized as "freedom fighters" by history.

In the late 1960's and early '70's, a small band of faithful Catholics did something similar against the modernist tanks that were rolling over the old Catholic way of life. They didn't see themselves as heroes, either. All they ever wanted to be was what their fathers and grandfathers had raised them to be—Catholics! Some called them "Traditional Catholics" but that's redundant, and they knew it. They were merely trying to hand down the Faith to their sons as it had been handed to them by their fathers.

In the name of Tradition they were banished from their parishes, castigated as "schismatic," and forced to live the old Faith in new catacombs. But they never forgot the words of their catechism: "You must be prepared to die rather than deny it." And so they remained for forty years—despite the spirit of Vatican II, the New Mass, and myriad novelties of an era marked by ecclesial and social chaos.

As for me, time moved on. Like many foolish young men I came to think of myself as a rebel. I didn't reject the traditional Catholicism I'd ingested with my mother's milk, but rather sought to set it aside. By the college years, I'd become weary of being different, of wearing the scapular, of dressing and acting in a way that just didn't fit in the hapless house that MTV built. But the Catholic giants of my childhood were tenacious in their pursuit, and I could not outrun them.

They finally ran me down in 1987 when I was a student at Christendom College. On a rainy day in the fall semester, my efforts to run away from my identity, my faith, the old Mass, and all of *them*, hit a wall guarded by a couple of Jesuits of the old school—Fr. Vincent Miceli and Fr. Edward Berbusse.

The rain was turning to sleet when I knocked on the old Jesuit's door. Like the sacrament I'd received at the hand of that saintly Archbishop ten years earlier, the memory of a general confession and another chance at redemption is something I will take to my grave.

There was a place called the Turnaround at Christendom. It was nothing more than a little clearing in the woods alongside a riverbank. There were those bluebird Northern Virginia days when the temptation to slip away to the Turnaround with a classmate or two proved too much. There on the banks of the Shenandoah with friends of the *Novus* persuasion, the old traditionalist convictions welled up from my soul once again. When it came to discussions of the Mass or the Council, the words of my father suddenly and most unexpectedly found their way back to my lips. Though I'd tried to outrun it, Catholic Tradition was overtaking me.

Benedicamus Domino!

If I have a "reversion story" worth telling, then, it's only that of the old warriors who'd defended the rightness of the Catholic cause with such clarity and conviction that even the toddlers at their feet grew into men eager to take up their standard—the standard of Trent, the standard of the Latin Mass, the standard of the old Faith. By the time I'd reached my twenty-fifth year, nothing else in life seemed to matter save tagging after that band of Catholic gentlemen and trying to earn the right to stand in their long shadows.

What about now?

I have six children of my own now, and I'd no sooner expose the precious gardens of their little souls—which God Himself has entrusted to my care—to the acid rain of the *Novus Ordo* than I would to the fare of Hollywood or MTV.

Why? Because down deep in my soul I fear it! Because I am no saint and thus cannot expose myself to it without fear of losing the Faith.

Eighty percent of Catholics under the age of fifty no longer believe in the Real Presence of Our Lord in the Eucharist.

Fifty-four percent of Catholics in America think abortion should be legal in all or most cases.

Forty-seven percent of Catholics think homosexual couples should be allowed to "marry," so long as no church would be required by law to perform such "marriages."

In Spain, less than thirty percent of Catholics attend Mass weekly. In France, just twelve percent. In Italy, less than half of the nation's Catholics. In the U.S., only thirty-two percent!

Why am I a traditionalist? Because statistics show that faith—and thus *salvation*—depends on it.

If this was true forty years ago, how much more so today! The last New Mass I witnessed illustrated the sheer folly of the entire *Novus* experiment in just a few heart-breaking seconds. I knelt down as Mass was about to begin. The church was mostly empty. A few old folks were still shuffling in as an enthusiastic lector busied himself dashing from pew to pew, shaking hands with the few Catholics who still bother to show up for Mass. No one was spared the honor, including me. "Hi there! Welcome to our worship service. I'm Bob!"

Hello, Bob.

Where have all the Catholics gone? There's nothing *novus* about any of this anymore. It's embarrassingly passé! It's man-centered rather than God-centered. It's emotionalism rather than worship. It stresses the communal meal rather than the sacrifice of Christ. It savors of Protestantism!

Is it any wonder, then, that our Holy Father should be distressed over the loss of Catholic identity throughout the world when even our Mass no longer looks Catholic?

Noting the universal decline in Mass attendance, Archbishop Albert Malcom Ranjith said in a recent interview: "We have to ask ourselves what happened in these churches. I do not think that this situation is attributable to secularization only. A deep crisis of faith coupled with a drive for *meaningless liturgical experimentation and novelty* have had their own impact."

Indeed they have, which is why traditional Catholics the world over avoid it like the plague.

Why do I attend the Traditional Mass? Because in good conscience, I cannot attend anything else. Millions have lost their faith since April 3, 1969, and while others who possess a stronger faith than mine might well be able to attend the New Mass and save their souls, it is also true that the Church is first and foremost for sinners, not saints, and this sinner clings to the Mass of our fathers as if his soul depends on it. Because, in truth, it does!

The traditional Latin Mass is gradually coming back into the life of the Church. Pope Benedict XVI noted in his motu proprio *Summorum Pontificum* that the old Mass had never been abrogated and that Catholics had a right to the Mass of the ages all along.

The Men in Black had the last word. *Deo Gratias!*

It's the Mass that matters. It always was and always will be–which is why the world, the flesh, and the devil have been waging war against the Latin Mass for five hundred years. *Lex orandi, lex credendi*–the law of prayer is the law of belief. How we pray is how we believe. Nothing on this earth is more important than restoring the Catholic Mass to its rightful place on the altars of sacrifice throughout the whole world.

It all starts with the Mass. It's the Mass that matters!

Michael Matt is the great-grandson of the founder of *Der Wanderer*, the grandson of the founder of *The Wanderer*, and the son of the founder of *The Remnant*. He's a graduate of Christendom College and the current Editor-Publisher of *The Remnant*–America's oldest traditional Catholic newspaper. With his wife and six children, he lives in St. Paul, Minnesota.

Brian Douglass

Views Along the Road to Tradition

I looked out the window as the plane began its descent into Lisbon. On the ground far below something like a shortened white banjo shone brightly in the setting sun. In fact, it was the reason that I was taking this flight. It was the new church at the Shrine of Our Lady of Fatima that would be dedicated the following morning. When I arrived at the shrine plaza, it was impossible to ignore the marked incongruity between this thoroughly modern structure on one end and the neo-classical basilica at the other. Recoiling from the visual affront and from the hoards of people, I left the plaza to walk the nearby stations of the cross. Here, among the peaceful oaks and olive trees, I prayed in silence broken only by lizards and birds. Out among the gentle breezes and rugged beauty, I could reflect upon the Mother of God and her visit to Fatima.

Had anyone told me in high school that one day I would not only be writing an essay about how I have been impacted by the Traditional Latin Mass, but also be considering a vocation to the priesthood, I would have thought that they were crazy. But, that is, after all how things happened. It is largely a story of my discovery of the Tridentine Mass and Catholic Tradition.

Lost in the Dark Wood

Unlike many who are attached to the Tridentine Mass, I did not live through the changes that swept the Church at the close of the Second Vatican Council. My immediate family and I converted to Catholicism through the RCIA program at our local parish in the 1990's. I have no memories of how things were before Vatican II; only dreams and ideas about how things could be. But, at times I feel like a detective who, upon arriving at the scene of a crime, must piece together what happened and determine how to proceed with the case.

Throughout middle school, I served at school and parish Masses, but I was never concerned much about growing in my faith. In high school, like so many of my friends, I fell in love with the modern world. I was especially fascinated by the logic and elegance of science and math. Religion, it seemed, was their exact opposite; it was all about "feelings" and didn't seem to offer concrete answers. One assignment for religion class, however, gave me my first ideas that perhaps there was more to this universe than what science could observe and math could quantify. Some Buddhist monks were making sand mandalas in town and as part of my assignment, I went to see them working. In their dress and actions, the monks seemed to reject the world; a foreign, but intriguing concept.

Fortunately, God can even use false religions to bring about His ends. I was attracted to Buddhism, not because I was consciously looking for truth, but because I was looking for novelty. But eventually the newness wore off and I moved on, next considering Islam. It was clear to me that Muslims, at least most of them, knew what they believed and were serious about it. For many, it was the focus of their lives—with a kind of devotion I hadn't seen in the Catholics of my experience. Mercifully, in the end neither of these religions fit with my Western mentality.

Then I discovered Eastern Orthodoxy. In the Orthodox rite I saw a Christian tradition which had elements of other-worldliness that interested me. Most importantly, through my study of the Orthodox I discovered the Church Fathers. Now I had found something! Here was philosophy, logic, reason, and beauty. Even though I stumbled upon these writings through Eastern Orthodox sources, I quickly saw that the teachings of the Fathers were very Catholic—though I had never been taught these things in my religious education classes. This new beauty, of the "highest things," transcended the material realm of the physical sciences and math

I had formerly relied upon, and it was an uncomfortable realization that took some getting used to.

Journey into the Light

That fall, I began my university career studying electrical engineering. I also began to study the various liturgies of the Church. Because of my interest in the Eastern Fathers, I was quite enthralled with the physical and linguistic beauty that I saw in the Divine Liturgies of the East. The sense of the sacred was so clear, and I was drawn to this expression of worship by something I couldn't quite put my finger on. I also studied more about the history and development of the Western Liturgy over the centuries. Comparatively, the Mass that I actually attended seemed drab and dull.

I had entered into the realm of what many would call *traditionalism*, though I don't like the term. My goal was and is simply to be a good Catholic, to obtain salvation, and to spend eternity with Christ in heaven. I had come a long way from my cafeteria-Catholic and borderline atheist days.

During my sophomore year of college, my university offered a class on hermits and monasticism. I half expected the class, like the honors program it was associated with, to be a hotbed of liberalism and strange ideas, but I was pleasantly surprised. The professor was a Catholic and a fan of G. K. Chesterton and J. R. R. Tolkien. Through this class, I filled in many gaps in my understanding of hermits, monasticism, and Eastern Christianity. But most importantly I discovered that I wasn't the only person on campus interested in such ideas. I picked up some new allies in the fight for sanity in the Cookeville area. I was also able to attend the Tridentine Mass most weekends as it was now offered in two locations within day-trip range from campus.

Junior year offered a chance to study abroad in Europe. My location of choice was Limburg in the south of the Netherlands at a school just a short train or bus ride from Aachen, Germany, home of Charlemagne. But all was not well in Europe, as I soon saw firsthand. The parish at which I attended Mass in the Netherlands was in a beautiful old Gothic masterpiece of a church. Sunday after Sunday as I rode my bike to Mass, the bells rang out across the town as they had for centuries. The inside of the church was well preserved and the high altar, while not used, was intact. But very few people came to Mass and I wondered why. The beauty of the church alone would have been enough to bring me to Mass week after week. In actuality, I found that Mass attendance was pitiful all around Europe, even in the churches of Rome herself!

The summer after I returned to the United States, I went with some friends to visit the Monastery of Our Lady of the Annunciation in Clear Creek, Oklahoma. The church was under construction so Mass was celebrated in a pole shed, a stark contrast to the magnificent architecture of the churches I had grown accustomed to in Europe. The holiness of the monks and the reverence of the faithful in the modest chapel contradicted the apathy and disinterest of the Europeans. As the monks quietly said Mass in the shadows of that metal building, the Oklahoma heat and the modern world disappeared: I felt like a visitor to medieval France. I hear it said that traditionalists are merely attracted to externals, but that is not what I observed in the simplicity of Clear Creek Monastery. It is something else in the Mass, not merely material or human, that calls to the very depth of our souls.

Through a bit of good timing, I was able to secure a spot in my university's study abroad program once again, this time for a year in Coventry, West Midlands, England. I knew little about Coventry other than that it was home to Lady Godiva and that it was close to Birmingham, which has many ties to both John Henry Cardinal Newman and J. R. R. Tolkien. I was also going to be relatively close to Oxford and London. This in itself was enough to close the deal.

I soon discovered that England was not the England of legend or even of *Brideshead Revisited*. It was more like George Orwell's *1984*. Just a short drive or walk outside of Coventry it was still possible to see fields and farms which must have changed little since Tolkien dreamed of the Shire. But a blackness hung about that was more oppressive than the soot that darkened the aged brick and stone. This disease went by many names, each describing a particular symptom: multiculturalism, political correctness, socialism, atheism, secular humanism, and many more. This was the disease which allowed such horrors as "homosexual marriage," abortion, and even human-animal hybrids to be considered morally acceptable. Modernism, defined as the synthesis of all heresies by St. Pius X, was the disease agent. The pestilent social conditions of England were shocking, even compared to what I had seen in other parts of Europe.

I could not escape the sense that I was at the scene of a crime. The evidence was apparent in the rampant immorality and in the ideas espoused by many of my peers and professors which could only lead to cultural suicide. Britain's mountains of petty little laws were a politician's dream come true. Not only were her citizens dependent on the government for everything from health care to, in many cases, day-to-day living expenses, but they were more than willing to swallow surveillance cameras and a multitude of restrictions. The English pubs, survivors of plague, Puritans, war, and the collapse of an empire, were no match for political correctness, socialized medicine, and global warming hysteria. These quintessentially English establishments were forced to close their doors in staggering numbers. England was self-destructing. And if Europe was in such a state, I reasoned, it would not be long before my home of Tennessee would face the same fate.

There were not many places in England where a sane man could find refuge, but I discovered two that proved immensely useful during my time in the Sceptred Isle: the Birmingham Oratory and Oxford. Each week, the Oratory in Birmingham offered a Mass according to the 1962 Missal. The simple chapel was packed and I was reminded of Clear Creek. It was an active parish and hardly a week went by without marches and prayers outside abortion mills, novenas, processions, Masses for the beatification of Cardinal Newman, and, of course, Benediction in the evenings. An authentic Catholic spirit was central to the social life of the community. Unlike most of the parishes in which I have attended the Tridentine Mass, the Oratorians had a long history, stretching back to Cardinal Newman's day. With an overwhelming sense of smallness, I found myself listening to the same Mass that both Newman and Tolkien knew and loved. The Church was universal indeed; beautiful and unbroken through time and space. How many had prayed in this very spot? There were still traces of the Shire here in England after all, and even men and women who were working to rebuild it in these dark and dangerous days.

If the Oratory and its community was a remnant of the Shire, then, for me Oxford was Tolkien's Rivendell. The dreaming spires were less than an hour away and the narrow, gray cobbled streets between the ancient walls soon became quite familiar. Nowhere else have I found the healthy mix of fun, beer, and intellectual sport as in the pubs of Oxford. All manner of good things for a Western man could be found in Oxford's shops, from old and obscure books, to caps and waistcoats, to the finest tobacco and pipes in the world. It was easy to think that here, at least, the corruption that was sweeping England was held at bay. But of course even in Oxford, the Modernists, leftists, perverts, and assorted nuts were able to hold court.

The Oxford University Newman Society, where I had the pleasure of attending several lectures, continued my education in Tradition. Topics varied, and included the prophetic nature of *Humanae Vitae* and *Summorum Pontificum*. Through the Newman Society I discovered Fr. Aidan Nichols and his recently published book *The Realm: An Unfashionable Essay on the Conversion of England*. Fr. Nichols lists a number of keys to the reclamation of England. One of these he terms the "re-enchantment" of the liturgy, arguing that the timeless beauty and enchantment of the Mass and the sacraments are her only hope. This, it seems to me, is an area where Traditionalists can make a valuable contribution to the defense of Western Civilization. I also attended a conference on the liturgy in Rome in which Fr. C. Frank Phillips, C.R., pastor of St. John Cantius parish in Chicago, presented a paper on integrating traditional aspects of Catholic culture into parish life; in other words, the *re-enchantment* of the liturgical year.

With ideas in my head of the central importance of not just the Mass, but also of Catholic culture to the health of Western

Civilization, I continued to search for this kind of living, vibrant, organic tradition. It was with this intent, in part, that I headed to the Middle East during Easter Holidays. When my plane landed in Istanbul, the minarets on the skyline showed me that I had entered another world that was practically as foreign as Mars–and I was still in Europe! For the next forty days, I traveled from Istanbul through Greece, to Israel, and on at last to Egypt.

The East did not disappoint. The churches where I attended Divine Liturgy were a beautiful and beloved part of the community. Some were perhaps centuries old and all were well used but well cared for. Carpets were worn from constant use, and the glass or plastic protecting icons was scratched and smeared from years of reverent kisses and loving touches. Churches were well maintained even in impoverished neighborhoods. But above all, tradition was preserved. It was a hopeful contrast to meager Mass attendance and dying parish life in Europe.

Modernists, as John Senior so forcefully points out in his collection of essays entitled *The Death of Christian Culture,* are defined by their quest for novelty, a quest that has emptied the churches of Christendom and vandalized Western culture. But in my travels I have seen glimpses of the depth and beauty of the Faith as it has been practiced unchanged for centuries. For me, the discovery of Tradition has been life-changing. It has provided me with a firm foundation for the defense of Truth, even here in East Tennessee. The only cure for the destructive maladies of Modernism is the Mass and a return to Catholic tradition. The importance of the Mass is not in the incense, the vestments, or even in the beautiful language of the prayers. The immense power of the Mass is simply the reality of Christ, present in the Eucharist.

Brian Douglass lives in Tennessee, where he is studying economics at Tennessee Technological University and discerning a vocation to the priesthood. In addition to travel, Brian enjoys gardening, fishing, shooting, and studying Catholic economic theory.

Anonymous

The Gate Called The Beautiful

And a certain man, who had been lame from his mother's womb, was being carried, whom everyday they put at the gate called the beautiful.

I

Beauty is a way to God; perhaps it is the most trodden by simple feet. Along the way of Beauty God does not drive souls to a conclusion; He the fairest of the Sons of men, lures them to His hiding place behind the clouds, within the sun.
–Fr. Vincent McNabb, *Thoughts Twice-Dyed*

When asked how it was that I ended up at Mass one Sunday, I can find only one answer that seems fitting. I am one of the lame that was laid at the gate of the beautiful. My own love and affection for beauty may have been better than most, yet still not sufficient to explain such a discovery. I had done nothing to merit the ability to understand the things I was shown and had not good sense to have sought them out. Therefore the lame man or the one lured is how I see myself coming to Mass, the victim of great mercy.

I was seventeen years old when I sat in class listening to the man that would take me to my first Mass a year later. A year after that, this same man would lay his hand on my back as water washed me clean of Adam's stain. This man was my English teacher, and besides being smart and poetic, he was kind. No doubt, his thoughtful classes and his voice, which I recall being enamored by, attracted me, but he snatched me with simple kindness in the end. I had lost my father only a few years prior, and my home was not a place where structure reigned. I was in need of a man to help me; God looks kindly on the fatherless, we are told—and I am convinced.

At the same time my mind and heart were filled with questions about the world around me. My best friend's parents had just filed for a divorce; my mother had just had a child with a man she was not married to, and he began living with us; and I had my first girl friend. The wreckage that comes from disordered love, the desperation of hearts wanting to find relief in any way possible, without regard for the consequences: this world is where I discovered beauty. It was in this state, as though lame, that I was brought to the gate.

My world was a modern suburban one. I was something of a middle-class music fan raised on MTV. Nirvana was the band of choice as I entered the seventh grade; I was learning Neil Young songs on the guitar when I was supposed to be at my studies. My father, when alive, was an avid collector of Arabic music and worked hard to mitigate my musical tastes. This was different from my friends; music was serious to him, and he had records in every nook and cranny of the house. After he died my mother had neither the ability nor the energy to stop me from listening to anything, and I spent most of my time in the basement with my records and a guitar. My friends took drugs quite often and fairly openly. Their parents had a practice of turning their heads and advising them not to get caught. I still had memories of my immigrant father telling me of the things he would do if I was involved in anything illegal—and, frankly, I was still scared of him even from the grave.

I am not quite sure why things were different for me. Why didn't I partake more often? Why was I so hesitant to participate at 3 A.M. as we walked the streets with our packs of cigarettes? Perhaps it was the tragedy of losing my father that gave me a certain gravity. Maybe it was God knowing that I was far weaker than the others. Most likely the latter, for I also had the good fortune of always getting caught for any infraction I committed, which was both humbling and preventative. I was the young man with shaggy hair, a love for music, cigarettes, alcohol—and little else.

I must say some more about my parents. They were both the products of their age. My mother was from a large Catholic family in a small Midwestern town. She was the youngest of seven and began moving away from the Church when the priest who frequently ate Sunday dinner at my grandparents' left the priesthood to marry a nun.

She met my father, a charming Arab trying to make it in London, towards the end of a jaunt across Europe; she was a liberated woman with her friend searching for an experience. My father was raised in Cairo in a lower middle-class family. His parents went through a nasty divorce when he was only three, and although he hardly spoke of it, he would say that he remembered it well. He was a Muslim, and he had a regard for the culture, but he had his own version of theology. He would poke fun at the American religion of feel-good sermons and the sentimentality of their prayers, yet he would also take the same tone when speaking of the Muslims in the community that sold alcohol yet talked about the importance of the Muslim rules and customs to live life well. He wanted his children to know that lying was wrong, that family was first, and that somehow the Muslim religion was a part of this reality.

So there I stood. My philosophy was confusing because I was confused. After my father died I tried to begin learning more about the Muslim religion out of respect for him. I went to the mosque on Fridays, I fasted and I prayed. The memory of my father changed drastically when I learned that he had been married to another woman. It is hard to say how a child comes to learn such things about their parents. I can say that I knew there was something wrong with my parents' marriage. After the death of my father, my mother didn't react like I thought she should. There was a tortured and hurt look that came to her face each time his name came up. They had been married for eighteen years when my father died, and she was dating only six months after his death. When I learned of the other marriage it seemed fitting; I was not surprised. I had no reason to believe that the Muslim religion, which said it was okay for my father to do this, was a good thing. Even my father had told me that he had trouble with one man being married to more than one woman. I believe he regretted his choice. Yet. to me, all the other options seemed just as incomplete. All that I saw of Christianity was just as unreasonable. More than anything, I wanted people to stop justifying everything; I wanted someone to tell me that my father was wrong—that things were not okay.

II

Sin alone is essentially hideous, ugly, loathsome. Yet the repented sin, as Magdalene's is, "fills the house with the odours of its sweetness."
  –Fr. McNabb, *Thoughts Twice-Dyed*

As I was beginning my senior year of high school, I was convinced to finish and get my diploma by the Headmaster and the kind English teacher togther. Since I had failed to meet the requirements for graduation my headmaster fashioned an elective for me to attain the necessary credits. This elective was an independent study in poetry that entailed meeting with my English teacher each morning with an anthology of poems.

Besides always listening to music, I also read and wrote poetry. The headmaster, prompted by my English teacher, gave me this class as a gift, hoping I would not disappoint. I am ever indebted to these two men, for during this semester class...something happened. To explain the miracle that takes place when someone begins to really learn—when the mind and heart expand and eyes open to something—would require a book that I have not the skill to write. If you have ever had a good teacher, an honest friend or a kind master that taught you something, you can relate. It is the kind of knowledge that is profitless and beautiful, useless and wonderful, which makes things like this happen. The poetry was rich soil for conversation and thought. There was no direction that was pointed out each day, we merely read and laughed and spoke, or occasionally said there is nothing to say about "that one" other than "It is sad and true." I would point out my favorite lines, and he would comment on them and sometimes point to his. I can remember spending the rest of the day ruminating upon the lines he called out.

The one virtue I found most infectious about the man was his obedience to being honest. He never attributed any virtue to himself, yet he always defended virtue. He never made excuses for himself. This made him very easy to talk to. As long as you could admit you were wrong, he would listen; if you approached him with a contrite heart, he was the easiest and gentlest of confessors. I had always been surrounded by people that made excuses. There had never been this resignation to weakness, there was never this honest answer before.

I had heard that he was a Catholic, but the idea confused me greatly. The only person I knew that was a serious Catholic was my aunt. She was always praying her rosary and talking about the end times. I frankly thought she was weird, if not crazy. I once mentioned this to my teacher, and he laughed and said that he thought he got along better with crazy people than the normal kinds.

There are moments during this time of my life that will always rest very clearly in my mind. The first is being at my girlfriend's house and finding a catechism. I flipped it open to the section on marriage. I read a passage from St. Paul that spoke of marriage. It spoke of divorce and the marriage of one man with one woman: I had never heard anything like this. I thought of my parents and all that had happened. I knew my teacher was married in the Catholic Church. What I read was all true, and I was sure that it was different from anything I had heard before. I was happy to think that true love made sense, but I was uncomfortable to think that my parents were wrong. It was uncomfortable–but good. It felt like sadness had a cause, like there was finally a reason things were so confusing.

I did not understand this then, but to forgive someone you need to understand that they have done something wrong. It is the greatest part of justice, the most beautiful part of having laws; they warrant real mercy. The only mercy I had seen before was laced with justifications for sin—which is really the denial of sin. It was as though the world I knew up to that point had a God who only forgave people because they didn't know that they were doing wrong. For instance, my father I was told to not judge because he "came from a different world," because he "grew up somewhere else." Yes, that is all true, but that doesn't mean that it is okay. For me to deal with my own sins and my father's, they had to first be admitted. The idea of universal laws, things unchanged and straightforward, meant that a God existed that forgave with a mercy more abundant and sweeter than ever before. I knew I had to forgive my father, but that meant admitting he was wrong because there are definitive lines that exist, and those lines existed for me, too.

I remember the phone call I made to my teacher soon afterwards. It was the first snowfall of the winter (though I forget the date) and I sat in my room staring out the window at the dusting flakes. I was nervous to call him, yet I knew he could help me. I told him that I was thinking about God and the Catholic Church. He said that we should meet and talk soon. He also said that I should pray and listen, for God speaks softly. He pointed out the gentle snowfall and how this was like that voice, not the storm.

When we met, he bought me a piece of pie that he insisted I get à la mode. We drank coffee and spoke. I told him that I thought I could not get married in any other religion than the Catholic. I said that I believed this was the greatest division between the Catholic Church and any other religion. I was probably trying to impress him with my enthusiasm that evening, but I did believe what I said. He agreed with me—but insisted that there was more. He said in the Muslim religion, God does not become man. He said the Catholic religion was different most of all because of the reality of that fact.

III

It was very soon after this meeting that I began attending Mass. For a young man who had grown up around Catholics and never heard people speak about the things I was now hearing,

I was not surprised to learn that this man helping me went to a Mass different from most Catholics I knew. The words of the phone conversation, the advice he gave me, never left me. My first Mass solidified these words in my breast. It was a Low Mass on a Saturday morning in a nearly empty church. There was no sermon, just the murmur of ancient prayers. He didn't give me any books to follow along. I just watched the choreographed dance of the priest and boy. I heard the quiet voice that I recognized from that first snowfall. I heard the same bells that had rung in my head as I learned there were rules, the bell that begs our attention. At moments I noticed the same silence that came about in his office as we read something that left us with our jaws locked. It fit in too many ways.

I knew this was beauty. Why I knew this I cannot say. This moment marked the beginning and end of many things in my life. I am still beginning most of these things and still trying to end many, too. It is my hope that you pray this young man shown such mercy will not disappoint the God who showered it upon him.

Dr. Kenton Craven

In the Sacred Cave

I believe that the impressions received by my eyes and ears give me adequate information about reality....I am afraid I have to admit it, I am a Stone Age man.
—Martin Mosebach, *The Heresy of Formlessness*

Benedict lived in caves. Elijah lived in caves. The Desert Fathers lived in caves. Athanasius almost surely lived in caves while fleeing persecution. And most importantly, the Word became flesh and was born in a cave. There may be something to cave dwellers.
—Brian Douglass

In the Cave with the Human Race

I am asked how I was led to the Traditional Mass, what attracted me, what of its beauty and mystery determined me to prefer it. I wasn't led to it; I was born into it; and as I hope to make clear, I do not find it possible or sane to leave it. It satisfies a hunger of the soul that cannot be answered by an argument. When I recently sought to distribute announcements for a Traditional Latin Mass, a priest snarled, "That is the Mass for those who confuse ritualism with real spirituality." This essay, I send to you, Father, in prayer.

The real answers to the questions lie at the base of my cerebral cortex in the deepest folds of ancestral and racial memory, in the true religious history of the human race, and in the Divine Mind as revealed to man in its most primitive origins and foundations. They lie in the simplest things: rock, water, wine, blood, dance, gesture, drama, story, worship, sacrifice, bells, incense, and prayer. If asked to point to things that are *like* the Mass, I would lead you to rock carvings in the Australian desert, rock circles in

Wyoming, the cave paintings of Lascaux, Stonehenge, the winter Dionysian festivals of Greece, secret ceremonies in kivas, the blood sacrifices of a hundred religions, the cries of shamans in deep canyons, the stepladder descending into a thousand-year-old pueblo, the chanting of *Beowulf* by a deeply moved Anglo-Saxon professor. In short, to many religious things in the human past and to no modern thing or things.

I am calling attention to this primordial dimension of my attraction to the Traditional Mass of the Roman Catholic Church because if I must answer how I came to prefer it, recent autobiography will not help. Later in the essay, I portray my days as an altar boy and suggest how they answer the question. Here I ask the prior question, *How do I prefer anything?* Only, the great teachers would say, because I am attracted to realities greater than myself. As in the epigraph quoted from Martin Mosebach, a German poet who loves the Mass, I wonder, *Why do I like anything?* When I get up in the morning, I can be struck with the wonder of air and light and the singing of birds in my garden. That is the first and most important level of wonder, which asks, *Where did all this come from? Who made these things? Who made me?* That is why the Baltimore Catechism begins with asking, *"Who made you?"* That is the level of deep knowing of primal things to which the Traditional Mass summons me at the very outset.

At the beginning of the Mass, the priest bows to say, "*Introibo ad altare Dei*, I will go unto the altar of God." In that verse from the Psalms is summed up the history of human hope before Christ. The prayers at the foot of the altar. "*At the foot of*"–I, the altar boy, and all who *hear* the Mass *bow down*. We have entered the secret place, the catacomb, the cave, the sanctuary, where the great transformation is to take place. The stone ledge in front of us has been consecrated as *the altar*. In bowing with David the poet of the psalm, we have entered the realm of poetic mystery and are ready to confess who we really are, sinners who need the saving power of the supreme sacrifice. That is our real identity as human beings, human beings in need, suppliants, crying out, "why do I go sorrowful, while the enemy afflicts me?" The priest, robed in sacred vestments, assumes the role of Christ, the true high priest, who now steps into the eternal event of the Sacrifice, in which He is both priest and victim. *"I will go to the altar of God, to God, who giveth joy to my youth."*

If I meditate on these verses of the beginning of the Mass and truly enter their spirit, I will have "heard" the Mass, as we used to say, in my soul. Prepared by purification and penance in the Mass of the Catechumens, I will be called to Consecration and Communion, the deeper mysteries, when bells call souls to God, as the poet Edward Dyson wrote. So they do, ringing us to attention.

The *Holy Sacrifice of the Mass* (as it is called in the documents of Vatican II) is a ritual sacrifice that takes place upon a hard rock in which are immured the remains of martyrs who died for the Faith. It is a drama enacted in a holy place designed to fulfill the requirements for true worship as outlined in Leviticus and echoed in the Epistle to the Hebrews. As a sacrifice, it sums up and completes all the sacrifices in all other religions, and as such a ritual it therefore includes ritual preparation, purification of the sacred tools and vessels, sacred vestments, a priest and an eternal priesthood created by God in the ancient Order of Melchisedech.[1] Like all sacred rituals, from those of the Australian aborigines to the temple customs of the Greeks and Romans, it takes the disciple out of ordinary time into sacred time, where what is done, the sacrifice of Christ on the Cross and the consecration of the Last Supper, are forever. As a devout Catholic from Madagascar told me, "In eternity, Christ is always dying on the Cross and Christ is always rising from the dead." It is this event that lies at the center of the Catholic religion and therefore of reality itself and which no *Novus Ordo* Mass I have ever seen evokes. The whole purpose of a ritual in any traditional religion is to evoke the sacred, to call it forth, to make present on the earth the meaning of

---

[1] The very best explanation of the Traditional Latin Mass is *The Latin Mass Explained* by Msgr. George Moorman, published first in *Our Sunday Visitor* in 1920 and now reissued in 2007 by TAN Books. I would strongly recommend starting classes for young people who are attracted to the Traditional Mass using this very fine book.

everything, the full significance of all creation, in the presence of angels and saints and Christ Himself. The difference between the ritual of the Mass and all other rituals, all of which prefigure it as St. Augustine teaches, is that it is the final, perpetual sacrifice toward which the whole history of the human race had been pointing. Imagine the millions of cold mornings in many cultures in which the suppliants stood before altars, hoping that the sacrifice of living things, including men, would bring the answers to their prayers in the flow of blood onto the earth, and felt their yearning for the salvation and truth that could only be realized in the Sacrifice of Christ. Now, here it is, and in this hushed and humble prostration before the final and absolute altar, the suppliants have the true hope that it is accomplished in the Mass.

When I teach literature, I tell students that they cannot understand answers until they experience the questions. Why the Mass? The Mass is the ultimate answer to the ultimate question of the disciples, "Lord, what must we do to be saved?" To enter it properly, we cannot be mere spectators. People who come and "look" at the "old" Mass often do just that; they take a look, are repulsed, and discard the thing. The point is that it is not to be looked at. As we used to say, and need to say again, we "hear" Mass, for in listening to the Mass we are hearing the Word not as words, but as *the* Word becoming Incarnate. That is why the Traditional Mass ends with the first chapter of the Gospel of John with its stark revelation that the *Logos*, the wisdom and being sought by the philosophers and cultures of the past, is here now, fully enacted.

To know the Mass, one must go deep within oneself–that is, beneath one's surface memory and personality–and return to things our race has left behind. A people that has lost reverence for food and eating (see Leon Kass, *The Hungry Soul: Eating and the Perfecting of Our Nature*) and hunting and planting is not going to "appreciate" the Mass. The Mass is eternal, and therefore sacred; not profane or ordinary. Even to be able to whisper a few of the ancient Latin phrases can be the entry to the sacred, which is a different dimension, as foreign to this culture as ordinary truths. For people who are negative on ritual and ceremony, including people for whom great and ancient stories hold no appeal, the Traditional Mass is not for them because religion is not for them. They have left the tribe: they are post-religion and thereby post-human. When I sometimes say the Traditional Mass is for the stupid, I mean that the initial reception of the Mass is at the level of *stupor*, the astonished or stupefied level, where we are least clever, most savage, most childlike, most prenatal, most tribal, most human. It is at that level of response when, on a frosty morning, the soul hears a bell. The blather about traditionalists wanting their "smells and bells" misses the point entirely. We want smells and bells because we are human, and if the Mass is about what it means to be wholly human in the sacrifice of Christ, who are we to suddenly become more "spiritual" than the Creator, who let the dust run through his hands and tasted the sweetness of wine? Today's young people who run from the Evangelicals toward the Hindus and Buddhists are saying something besides "a pox on your chapter-and-versing"; they are saying *they want religion*. If they find it in the Japanese tea ceremony, that says something about the nature of their seeking. It reminds me of composer Olivier Messiaen finding the depths of the "*Mystère de la Sainte Trinité*" in the sounds of hedgesparrows and bulbuls.

Therefore what I have to say about the Mass is elementary for ordinary, stupid, Stone Age minds. A wild and crazy anthropologist, John Greenway, in *Down Among the Wild Men* (1972), said that when Pope Paul VI suppressed the old Mass and gave us the Modernist substitute for it, he destroyed the Catholic *religion*. He destroyed the central religious rite, ritual, mystery, and practice that the Catholic laymen and priests of England and elsewhere risked their lives for. It is the center, just as certain rituals among primitive peoples form the center of their visions of reality, their deep sense of community. And until the old Mass is fully restored, I believe, the Catholic Church will continue to burble about "community" without really experiencing it and to founder in a modernism that denies the religious nature of man.

Love in the Ruins

In *The Sacred and the Profane: The Nature of Religion* (1957), Mircea Eliade saw that all religious rituals connect heaven and earth. They establish that connection by telling the one true story which takes place outside ordinary time in sacred time, which is "infinitely recoverable, infinitely repeatable," and "ontological." Though Christianity profoundly completes and transforms the mythical time of all other rituals through the Incarnation, bringing heaven to earth (*et incarnatus est*) rather than straining after the ethereal beyond, it is a ritual nevertheless. To neglect this dimension of the Mass and why it is perfectly suited for our human minds and hearts is to pass over the primal facts and enter into arguments over liturgy that lie, thankfully, outside the stone borders of this essay in the Misty Lands of Nuance, where no Stone Age man dare go.

In the Cave with Stone Age Men

Permit me to continue this meditation on the Traditional Mass with some thoughts of another Stone Age man, Hilaire Belloc. Like me, Belloc would say there is nothing original in what he has to say about the Mass. His Neanderthal observations struck him in the midst of some very primal things in his own life–mad, medieval things like vows, pilgrimages, self-inflicted pain, and getting utterly lost in the Alps. Picture young Hilaire Belloc, a hundred years ago, visiting the church in the French village where he was born. He kneels to pray before the high altar and has one of those wonderful moments the truly young and brave sometimes have had in Christian civilization:

> I was quite taken out of myself and vowed a vow there to go to Rome on Pilgrimage and see all Europe which the Christian Faith has saved; and I said, "I will start from the place where I served in arms for my sins; I will walk all the way and take advantage of no wheeled thing; I will sleep rough and cover thirty miles a day, and I will hear Mass every morning; and I will be present at high Mass in St. Peter's on the Feast of St. Peter and St. Paul."

Belloc's story, recounted in *Path to Rome: A Portrait of Western Europe Before the World Wars* (1902), is a crusty, delightful, odd tale of a journey on foot across much of Europe, a different tale from a different time, before Europe became modern, a time when he could expect to attend Mass in any village in any country. And, yes, a time in which he could rightfully expect to hear the sound of church bells on his way to a Mass that was always the same: *i.e.*, a universal (catholic) Mass for mankind. Belloc reflects on the "pleasing sensation of order and accomplishment which attaches to a day one has opened by Mass." He attributes this sensation (yes, sensation, not something intellectual or merely cerebral) to four causes:

> 1. That, for half an hour at the opening of day you are silent and recollected, and have to put off cares, interests, and passions in the repetition of a familiar action....
> 2. That the Mass is a careful and rapid ritual... [that can] catch you up (as it were) into itself, leading your life for you during the time that it lasts....
> 3. That the surroundings incline you to good and reasonable thoughts, and for the moment deaden the rasp and jar of that busy wickedness which both working in one's self and received from others is the true source of all human miseries. Thus the time at Mass is like a short repose in a deep and well-built library, into which no sounds come and you feel yourself secure against the outside world.
> 4. And the most important cause of this feeling of satisfaction is that you are doing what the human race has done for thousands upon thousands upon thousands of years. This is a matter of such moment that I am astonished people hear of it so little. Whatever is buried right into our blood from immemorial habit that we must be certain to do if we are to be fairly happy...and, what is more important, decent and secure of our souls. Thus one should from time to time hunt animals, or at the very least, shoot at a mark; one should always drink some kind of fermented liquor with one's food–and especially upon great feast-days; one should go upon the water from time to time; and one should dance on occasions; and one should sing in chorus. For all these things man has done since God put him into a garden and his eyes first became troubled with a soul.

Finally, Belloc concludes:

Now in the Morning Mass you do all that the race needs to do and has done for all the ages where religion was concerned; there you have the sacred and separate Enclosure, the Altar, the Priest in his Vestments, the set ritual, and all that your nature cries out of in the matter of worship.

Love in the Ruins

In the twenty-two days it took for Belloc to fulfill his vow, the Mass was as present as the mountains and rivers. Like mountains and rivers, the Mass is solid and set. Humans perennially have one response to any departure from ritual: horror at blasphemy. It is not my purpose to recycle the modern phenomena of either liturgical abuses or liturgical "experimentation." I will simply repeat what I have said above: they, like the people who do them, are post-religion and thereby post-human. This is a metaphysical and anthropological, not a moral, judgment. The human race has not liked such things. Belloc reaffirms these fundamental truths about ritual and ceremony: we want them, we want them to be careful, and we want them to be sacred, and we want them to be secret and devout and predictable.

To be those things we want them to be, as Belloc's observations make clear, extra-personal and outside ourselves, for through them we are brought up against a reality that is not of our own making, a reality that is objective, not subjective. In short, we want something holy. Holiness, like the sacred, is a universal human thing. All peoples until the modern era had concepts of sacred spaces; ceremony; hierarchy; sacred art, music, poetry, dance, and stories; and sacred emotions, that is, sets of emotional responses reserved for worship. It has often been noted that when the Russian Patriarch Nikon made a few minor changes in the Orthodox liturgy of Russia, including changing using three straightened fingers instead of two for making the Sign of the Cross, the Old Believers left in schism. It is easy for modern historians to make fun of such things, but perhaps they miss the point: the deep habits and practices of religion are close to people's hearts and imaginations, for religion is lived through the imagination. As St. Thomas sees it in the *Summa Theologica*, the mass of mankind knows the mysteries through symbols. The connection between emotion and imagination is most profoundly imprinted on the psyche when we are young, and volumes of psychoanalysis have been written on the catastrophic effects on human beings when those connections are suppressed or lost, like the Aborigines found depressed and starving because their totem pole, their connection to the world above, had broken. Belloc's *Path to Rome* portrays a healthy soul fed on the Mass and the sane Christian culture that grew from it; yet he was deeply aware that he was writing about a culture imperiled.

The terrors of the lost, isolated, despairing psyche were the subject of much early modern literature, from T. S. Eliot's *The Wasteland* to the novels of Evelyn Waugh and Walker Percy. When I first saw the wrecking of the churches and the Mass, I felt as if something was being ripped from me. My inner space (see Gaston Bachelard, *The Poetics of Space*) was suddenly lacking in its furniture, its sounds and smells, its music and all-important shadows. All was laid bare and made sterile. In reading Belloc's account of his pilgrimage, I am struck by his assumption that the solidity and permanence of the holy and permanent things will continue in the Mass and the churches of Europe. His plain, ordinary workaday Catholicism was anchored in the mysterious sacraments. It is enough for him that they are there and he can turn to them and be succored.

In the Cave with the Angels

Memory, as St. Augustine taught us powerfully, is where we live and where our imagination, the heart of our hearts, is shaped. This essay on the Traditional Latin Mass is a testimony from memory, and a carving in rock, like those pictures the Aborigines of Australia left in the deserts many thousand years ago. This I tell you so that you will have no grounds for complaint; I am not a theologian, much less a canon lawyer or liturgist. What I know is *story*, and that is what the Mass is to me, not *a* story but *the* story, the memory of all the things we really can know. Recently I played with the idea that the Mass could be a constitution for a Christian society, that it set forth all we believe in, as the poets used to say, *an action*. Come to think of it, that is what I was taught in college, that the Mass is an action, a sacrifice. For a poet or story lover, it is the action at the very center of being itself, of all creation, and analyzing it in bits and pieces is as useless as literary criticism that hacks away at a great story and destroys it.

Love in the Ruins

And though I have diligently read many books on the old Mass, I am not a politically correct traditionalist. I do not obsess about how many candles are on the altar and would just as soon hear the Mass in the galley of a sailing ship by the light of whale oil or on the deck of a battleship than hear several traditionalists fussing about the rubrics. So please consider the first two sections of this little piece as a clearing of the decks for my story, which is for the young, for young men and women who love good old things, like jackknives, tools, black powder rifles, grape vine swinging, apple pan dowdy, birds, animals, rivers, and frosty mornings on the trail. For my grandchildren. For, in short, young people who live at least some of the time in the real world and are susceptible to real poetry and real fiction when they see it—to a speech by Shakespeare or stories by John Buchan, rimes by Chesterton, songs by Belloc, and old things, worn things, remembered things, like a worn Roman coin I found in Ephesus, inscribed *Theodosius*, the last great Emperor of a united Christendom. That last word, Christendom, is a test. If it swells your heart with hope, you have been well taught; if not, begin your real education now.

What was it like, back then?—you ask—*when you served Mass?* Think snow blankets crusted on coal cars. Smell coal or coke smoke from every chimney and all the locomotive smokestacks on the glistening tracks. Hear church bells ringing the Angelus over the railroad yard. Feel knees on cold marble steps. I am twelve, there's a war against Communism in Korea, flatcars carry shrouded tanks and artillery, troop trains roll through the station every day, miners are threatening to strike, Eisenhower is president, Pius XII is Pope, obedience is the norm in the churches and schools, movies are about cowboys and courage, I've never even heard the word homosexual, almost no one has television on my side of town, we carry our marbles in little cloth sacks and shoot in the alleys, a steelie will crack a regular marble if you're fast enough, and when the priest holds the Host up above his head you say, "My Lord and my God!" and something changes in your soul. It's 1952. The Mass begins like all good tales in the hours just before dawn, and it ties together heaven and earth. I get up in the winter-cold dark and peer out the window at the only world I know: the railroad, the silvery lights blinking against Stony Ridge on the other side of the rail yards, heavy fog rolling down the slopes. Muffled up, canvas newspaper bag on my shoulder, I step onto our high porch and hear below the random clank and groan of coal cars, the hissing of steam from the switch engines, the long blues-rich moan of the freight train pulling the long grade from the East River Valley. A switch engine bell rings wildly as it races for the roundhouse, shift almost done. I am alone, shuffling down the hill. Everything is silent between the steaming hisses of the trains. I pass Sacred Heart Church and make the Sign of the Cross. God is *In There*, behind stone walls two feet thick, in the silences, in the Tabernacle where He has rested through the night. Faith flickers in me like the red sanctuary lamp, which I know is there also, hanging from golden chains. I remember that I have not been to Confession for a few weeks. Guilt is like Sister Assumpta looking over my shoulder. Her stiff habit smells of starch. "He dreams too much, he doesn't pay attention, *Ach Ja*." It's true. I don't. Perhaps that is what sin is, not paying enough attention. If I could pay perfect attention...but I don't want to, I still want the dreaming. A traditional Catholic church is a long dream, the memories of the Body of Christ stretching all the way back to Bethlehem: it stirs dreaming and prompts dreaming in the soul. The dreaming of sacramental moments, which formed the poetic imaginations of Catholic poets from Hroswitha through Cervantes and Dante to Waugh and O'Connor. I long for such moments, when I am alone in a world of images: this morning, walking the empty streets where the street lamps reflect off the wet black macadam, and carrying the newspapers to people still asleep in their homes. I stop in a deserted hotel lobby to cover my bag with plastic and catch the headlines. "Korea: Fierce Snow Slows Fighting Along The 38th Parallel," the headline says, and there is a photo of an army truck buried in snow. Here and there, a single car makes tracks in the white streets.

Love in the Ruins

All the papers out, I turn into the church for the seven o'clock Mass. Entering the church in those days was indefinably and, as we now say glibly, awesome. It was a different cosmos. The columns, the arches, the apse, the murals and statues and paintings—and the silence!—let you know that you had truly entered God's house, a different realm of being. Above the nuns bowed in prayer and the veiled Sicilian ladies murmuring their rosaries before Mary's side altar, a sparrow flutters around the painted nave. I rush into my cassock and surplice and hear Father pounding down the aisle; after his brusque greeting, I am busy lighting candles and carrying out the cruets. Father murmurs the prayers as he takes the vestments of the day from one of the drawers, and when he is finished he bows down on the cabinet and prays before we go out to the altar. It's just me today, Joey didn't show and he will be in trouble when Sister Innocentia nails him at the school door. I kneel on the right side and begin the responses, *Ad Deum qui laetificat juventutem meam,* to God who giveth joy to my youth. The Mass goes quickly and slowly, there are times when I have to be alert to every motion to ring bells, hold Father's vestment, change "the book" from one side to the other, bring the water and wine, say the *Suscipiat,* hold the paten for Communion. But there are oceans of silence in between, when I am as alone as I was on the paper route, now in a different world of smells and sounds and emptinesses. I hear the coughs and the rattling of rosary beads from the parishioners, the scuffling feet of late comers and early goers, the cheeps of the sparrow. *We are all alone together in the Mass.* Above me there are the four angels in the panels on either side of the Tabernacle, each looking straight out into the silence, each holding a scroll on which there is golden writing edged in black:

I have loved, O Lord
The Beauty of Thy House
And the Place
Where Thy Glory Dwelleth!

These words from the Psalms burned into my mind. I knew they spoke of the Tabernacle, where all our attention was directed. Kneeling where I do, I am always watching the Tabernacle door and the veils that enclose its secret space, as if I can catch a glimpse of something inside. I know that only the consecrated hands of the priest can touch it or the holy vessels. *Dwelleth.* It is a word that says something that I cannot begin to form in my mind, but it touches deep spaces, as do the scrolled letters. *Beauty.* This place, this church, is the most beautiful thing I know, there is nothing else like it in the town. Kneeling there my imagination is shaped on every side, radiating from the Tabernacle outwards. I can still hear the noises of the railroad, the bells and whistles and the clanking of coal cars and the rolling wheels slipping on the snowy tracks. I can hear traffic now, as delivery trucks awaken the town. Here, inside the Story, we are already awake, kneeling before the Creator, bringing in the day. *Out there*, nothing would matter without the *In Here*. That is the secret of what it was like back then, when the Mass and the Church sat at the center of our imaginations and touched all things with grace and beauty. No matter what I see in my life, I will see it through the imagination formed in a world in which the Mass touched all. The Last Gospel, *"In the Beginning was the Word,"* moved me as deeply then as now. I shudder to think of a world without that hush and murmur, that reverence and those arresting silences of the true liturgy of heaven and earth, where the Sacred meets everything else, in the words, and in the immense silences between the words. People speak of the moments after the Big Bang. They have no idea of the moments after, *"And the Word Was Made Flesh, and Dwelt Among Us."* But that is where we really live, where we kneel at the altar rail like baby chicks, our mouths open, waiting for Mother Church to feed us.

Dr. R. Kenton Craven, a scholar-in-exile, lives in Sparta, Tennessee.